TAPESTRY OF POETRY, PATHOS AND LOVE

TAPESTRY OF POETRY, PATHOS AND LOVE

One Man's Unique Strategy to Elevate Optimism
In His Cancer-Stricken Wife

JACK STEVENSON

To my best childhood friend and for fifty-five years my loving and precious wife, Debbie, without whom I would be as lost as a grain of sand on the beach. By our Lord's design we are the embodiment of true soulmates, together in this world and the next.

And to our closest friends and family, especially my son and daughter, Michael and Jaime, who provided love, encouragement and enduring support before, during and after our joint challenges with initial and recurrent breast cancer treatments.

The expression "it takes a village" truly represents a most relevant description of the importance of love, prayer and continuous connections to both spiritual and emotional needs of all undergoing serious medical challenges. We are blessed and humbled to be denizens of such a village.

"Humor and pathos, tears and laughter are, in the highest expression of human character and achievement, inseparable." James Thurber

TABLE OF CONTENTS

ACKNOWLEDGEMENTS

My worry here, as is likely the case with many authors wishing to thank the people most instrumental in their journey of writing and publishing a book, is that I miss someone important, and risk hurt feelings. This journey began from diagnosis, extended over the length and breadth of Debbie's treatments, and continued throughout the aftermath including the two-plus years of my publishing effort. Over the course of Debbie's cancer, two iterations four years apart, there were many circumstances where friends, acquaintances and family played a major role uplifting both me and Debbie. I freely admit to memory lapses. As a man in my early seventies, that is not unusual. Yet, I am not letting the fear of missing someone dissuade me from taking a leap of faith that any omissions will be overlooked under such stressful circumstances of extended cancer caregiving. And further taxed during the two-plus year publication process. Similarly, Debbie had many encounters of which I knew nothing and therefore cannot extend a thanks to these friends. My intention is to express my gratitude to the people with whom I came in contact, distinct from Debbie's experiences. After all, while this book is about my unique journey, this odyssey's purpose was entirely dependent on and intertwined with every breath Debbie took, every day. So, if your name is missing, please sympathize with my cerebral limitations.

First and foremost, my gratitude to my Lord God cannot be adequately expressed. Attempting to write a poem per day for ninety some days, dealing with the subject as dark as cancer in an effort to uplift the mood and positivity of my dear wife, Debbie, covered me with a measure of anxiety and self-doubt. Yet, I am convinced that words and thoughts came to me in ways I cannot reasonably explain. Without the Lord's whispering frequently to me on a daily basis, I likely would have faltered. Distinct from this was my daily time of prayer during which I laid bare my full and open heart and soul to Him. Of course, I prayed for direct healing of my dear wife. I prayed for insights to being a better caregiver. I asked that the full array of medical science be brought to our medical team of four physicians. I prayed that I might be up to the task of achieving a sort of nirvana of positivity, never letting down my guard to display anything but optimism and tirelessness in pursuit of my daily tasks to care for Debbie and Sweetie. I prayed that Debbie would seldom, if ever, become weakened or bereft of her lifelong penchant for inner strength, peace and gentle spirit; traits for which she is known. I prayed for mental tranquility for both of us. In all of these prayers, the Lord had my back, for which I extend all honor and glory.

While I viewed my task in Debbie's recurrent treatment to being her Rock of Gibraltar on which she could lean for comfort, love and encouragement, looking back, at times the opposite occurred. Her eternal optimism, living life moment to moment became inspirational to me in many ways. She literally hummed her way throughout this period. (see Hum for Joy) I cannot express with precision how my daily poems appeared to generate a sort of symbiosis with her daily joy. I simply felt an elevation of mood that filled me with just enough "juice" and excitement to continue writing for another day. My gratitude to and for Debbie remains an immutable reality.

My phenomenal children, Michael and Jaime, without exception unceasingly devoted time, energy and offered thoughtful advice to both me and their mom. Each of many telephone conversations over the nearly two years of treatments filled our emotional cups with love, tenderness and understanding. I never ended talks with either not feeling more positive and uplifted than at the start. I grew closer to each during the darkest part of my life. This is significant given that neither lived remotely close, especially Jaime in Alaska. Yet, both made special efforts to visit during which many hugs and kisses were exchanged. Our family has never been short of love and hands-on affection. I was and still am filled to the brim with love and gratitude to both Jaime and Michael who went the extra mile for both Debbie and me during troubled times.

We have all heard the expression "it takes a village," to accomplishment seemingly impossible objectives. I know there were many friends, some acquaintances, who became close friends during the year after diagnosis. Some gave words of comfort and encouragement, others sincere love and prayer. There were many cards, phone calls, and in some cases actual presents, the latter being the most unexpected but highly prized for the thoughtful presentations. And then there were the many meals offered throughout the nine months. I had taken over all cooking, so it could be said that I was the most appreciative for this. Yet, my temporary career as head chef could not compare with the gourmet meals we received and enjoyed, the three of us, when they arrived.

Beginning with that, yet not wanting to select a favorite gourmet chef, I still must mention the excitement that each delivery engendered within our small family unit. On one occasion Lou and Gerry Nowak prepared food that took a full week for us to consume, complete with wine and Turkish desserts, a vestige of her family history. We also enjoyed devouring myriad wonderful dishes from Linda Schlesinger, Judy Landolt-Korns, Ellen Curran, Valerie McMullan, Helen Smith, Lars and Jean Larson, Bob and Marlis McKay, Carol Williams, Linda Tiani, James Audi, Debbie Williams.... So many offered the following "if there is anything you need, don't hesitate to ask..." Again, I apologize If I missed anyone.

Yet, the one reply I wanted so desperately to speak, I simply could not. "Well, you know I have taken over the cooking, and it really isn't my strong suit." I simply could not imply or ask for personal Doordash delivery services. It didn't seem right. Perhaps my readers might file that away for future relevance. The days of a caregiver are fuller than most can imagine, sort of like a working mother who comes home and has to cook dinner, do the laundry, bathe the kids. You see what I mean. I must thank Debbie and Sweetie for never once complaining about my learning to cook on the fly. No one gained weight, but no one lost a pound either, or did I dream that?

On the flip side of the support coin were the numerous people who provided the emotional bedrock undergirding our months long ordeal. Some that I recall being most active include my brother Thom and his wife Karen, cousin Lynn Robinson, Cathy Patterson, John Lalli, Dennis and Jane Dress, Bob and Marlis McKay, the Larsons-Jean and Lars, Helen and John Smith, James Audi, Bud and Bev Elzey, Connie and Greg Fries, Debbie and Rich Dryden, Mike Swaney (Debbie's bother), Sara Swaney, Pat Smith, Terry and Brenda Fowler, Shawna Kivanc (niece), Jerry and Kathy Carter, Jim and Kate Melesky, Karen and Bob Lane, Sheila Baranzyk, Nancy MacDonald, Ellen Curran, Nancy Smith, Betsy Mikkelson, Debbie's kind college roommate Tana Cortese and all of my high school friends with whom I reconnected at our 50th reunion. Much gratitude to any I failed to mention.

To Philip Russell, Debbie's hairdresser for over twenty-five years who sadly sheared her hair after chemotherapy began to take her hair for both occasions of cancer. And then as needed as it grew back, he trimmed to keep it neat, albeit very short. He refused to take payment for any of his work over these extended treatment cycles. Not only was he kind and empathetic, he was a terrific listener and conversationalist, at a time when such qualities meant even more than during normal times. A true friend to both of us in all respects.

To the entire Garden Club of Fairfax, Virginia (100-year-old club for women) of which Debbie is a member, and I, one of four male honorary members. Again, for me, I routinely received kind-nesses or had direct knowledge of such from members such as Carol Williams, Linda Schlesinger, Carole Allred, Lisa Johnson, Linda Tiani, Donna Moulton, Claudia Lewis, Diane Wilkerson, Johanna Rucker, Jackie Anderson (passed away from an extended bout with cancer-a sorrowful loss a short time after Debbie competed her treatment) and others where my memory lapses. All the gifts were memorable and thoughtfully selected from books to jewelry, coffee mugs and plaques all with inspirational messages. See one such beautiful gift, a blanket, associated with my poem "Dainty Headwraps."

Our joint experience with two cancer diagnoses confirms just how important the medical team is both in terms of actual performance of surgeries as well as participatory deliberations leading to treatments. In this regard, we subjectively award 100 stars, based on a maximum of 10 for our incredibly gifted, empathetic and high-performing team consisting of Dr. Laura Mauro (medical oncologist); Dr. Robert Cohen (oncology breast surgeon); Dr. Ashish Chawla (radiation oncologist) and finally Dr. Alex Mesbahi (reconstruction plastic surgeon). This team that collaborated on some difficult issues concerning Debbie's somewhat rare type cancer were always available for us to field questions, provide recommendations, and continue to follow progress long after treatments concluded. As I never missed any appointments with Debbie, I can say without reservation just how instrumental and impactful individually and collectively these professionals were. And oh, my goodness, for each, a more amiable personal deportment could not be found anywhere.

I would be terribly remiss if I did not express my thanks to the wonderfully talented digital artists I employed to produce some 140 images for me. For the first fifteen months Ms. Sheryl Chieng (Malaysia-https://guru.com/freelancers/Sheryl-cse) extraordinarily painted eighty-six pieces. Most artists I noted specialize in one type media. Sheryl did everything from cartoons to portraits for me. I treasure her patience with a first-time self-publisher and her continued responsiveness sans any hint of defensiveness when I occasionally asked for revisions. When I expanded my vision to one illustration per poem, I discovered the online multi-platform Fiverr.com. There, I used eighteen different artists in many specialties hailing from ten countries. I am indebted to the following who provided these original digital paintings for me, the numbers shown in parenthesis along with their country of origin. I am only listed them by their internet or advertised user name along with the number of paintings, in case anyone reading this might want to avail of their service: Venborne (22-Kasmir/India); Arifzoeli (16-Indonesia); Elenaprovik (9-Belarus); Marylicm50 (1 France); Prasetiadi (3 Indonesia); Nariel_enii (1 Russia); Kyriakizou (1-Greece); Fezwerke (1-Singapore); Pixdesignking (3- Bangladesh); Sabartstudio (1-Indonesia); Anzonart (2-Bangladesh); Usamaqayyum968 (Pakistan); Ramomonitabyro (3-origin unknown).

Lastly, to my extraordinarily talented and highly professional responsive designer, Ghislain Viau of Creative Publishing Book Design, who worked tirelessly days, nights and even weekends to deliver the most exceptional designs. He far exceeded his commission and my high expectations with well thought out creative recommendations that he presented with easy to grasp points. He garnered my trust from day one. As a one-time self-publisher, fearful of not achieving personal expectations, discovering and working with Ghislain punctuated the end of the long process with a calming sense of excitement and satisfaction I will always treasure.

INTRODUCTION

*T*apestry *of Poetry, Pathos and Love* is a love story told in verse and woven from the threads of passion, empathy, and persever-ance. Occasional humor contributes to further lighten the mood. Prayerfully, this is the last chapter in a victorious family epic exalting the character, strength and courage of my dear wife, Debbie, now a two-time breast cancer survivor.

This compilation of original daily poems captured my mien as I cared for Debbie during her second act of treatments for breast cancer in 2019. She survived four years, a blessing, before recurrence. The shock of its return took a heavy toll on her, me and her 101-year-old mom living with us. Publishing this book became a natural extension of composing several score of poems to permanently enshrine the ups and downs of this trial to our physical and mental psyche. And share that story with the many families and friends who rendered incredulous loving support throughout the ordeal as well as others who are or have served as caregiver to a loved one with cancer. This story includes more than "cancer empathy." Rather, it gives rise and expression to the backstory of our life together. It highlights times before and after marriage, encompassing fifty-nine years beginning when she saw "this cute boy my age and did not recognize, riding his bike down the street." We were both thirteen. An occasional walk through the positive times of our life, re-sharing memorable events, seemed like an excellent form of daily therapy I attempted to capture and share with Debbie. This history is foundational to understanding me, my motivation, purpose and state of mind that guided my actions throughout Debbie's trials of battling cancer.

The inspiration to write the daily poems in section one of this book grew from two immutable personal truths. One, the Lord wired me with certain traits and my mom advanced that coded essence to inculcate a passion to exercise every fiber of my being to becoming the best I could be in every pursuit whether physical, cerebral, or emotional. Mom stressed that success aggregated around intentions and effort, not necessarily results alone. I believe I was already "wired" to receive and use mom's advice. From a small child I had always put forth maximum effort into all activities. Sometimes even with good results. Exhaustion formed the pattern; no reserve "to fight another day." I learned that we each have been provided by the Lord with our own set of unique gifts. That one of mine centered on the capacity to "give everything" to one event and yet, still be able to come back the next day and reproduce an equal or nearly equal measure of effort, results aside. Subject only to limitations of the physical body. Of course, this discovery did not occur overnight, but due to my early adolescent competitiveness in sports, this "secret sauce" simmered for a while, bubbling into reality over time.

I came to feel that each event, task or problem would yield to this recipe. Of course, not all did, and I learned from that. Mom advocated these priorities above others that many might argue were far more important. Okay, I "hear" you thinking what about attributes such as integrity, kindness and generosity? I'm not saying these were never mentioned, but mom was a World War II bride, married at nineteen. I arrived three years later, following two brothers. By many standards, mom was still growing into adulthood. In all she raised four boys, under amazingly tough conditions, including non-acceptance by my father's family. I am still in awe of how she coped and stand as evidence of her positive influence. You see she lived daily *by leaving everything on the field*. And she lived honesty, kindness and generosity. I like to believe I absorbed some of that too.

As I matured, my personal hard wiring added results to the formula. In my mind, I anticipated only excellent results if I applied rule number one. This lesson took time. I grew and matured from a cocky adolescent on the outside, a defense mechanism protecting fragile and damaged sensibilities, absorbed unconsciously from an abusive father and third child syndrome to a more people-caring path in life. Debbie's complete non-judgmental unconditional love persona rubbed off much of my defensive nature, allowing my inner good to surface. This redefined "me" perceived the possibility and obligation to leave everything of me "on the field." Elevating her, caring for her, loving her even more demonstrably became kind of a personal test. If not now, when? We were over seventy years old. Would I have another chance to go beyond myself, to do everything in my power, to leave nothing undone or unspoken that conveyed my deepest love, respect and admiration for my best friend in life? My presumption naturally acknowledges the existence of this inner good. I consider that I'm still a work in progress.

The second, equally important reason for undertaking these poems rested on my deep conviction to lift up Debbie, to elevate her morale, levels of optimism and well-being to a plane of confidence where every day she began with a "I got this" attitude. Yet, I realized a fallacy in this presumption. As a deeply independent "glass half- full" person, Debbie's charisma oozed positivity before, during, in-between, and after combat with her cancer. She could have fought and won against this cancer demon without me. Did she not persevere throughout her first cancer trial, and a life married to a Soldier who moved frequently (15) and with the loneliness and worry of deployments approximating five years? Most assuredly!

Know first that these poems came to me daily, inspired by the Lord. Of that I am certain. Some months later, as I began the publishing process, I barely recognized many of these poems. Where did the words come from? Certainly, from my innermost core of feelings and emotions, with a spiritual presence guiding my fingers on the keyboard. I won't posit having no input nor effort. Yet, the writing should not have been this easy nor quick. Nearly all of the poems, six verses or less, I penned in no more than two hours, before breakfast each day; typed and cut to greeting card size, then pasted in the card I chose to present. Some compositions nearly wrote themselves in a mere fifteen minutes or less. On those occasions, I spend the extra time working on some of the longer more complex verses.

I did not begin with the intent for a daily poem. A daily card, yes. During the lead up to and through Debbie's surgical phase, I occasionally included a poem. Debbie's reaction, in keeping with that of past poem presentations, included a radiant beaming smile that lit up my internal fires. I mused if I might extend myself and attempt a poem per day. And so it began, after her first chemotherapy, and continued to the end of her twice daily radiation in November 2019. Longer more intricate-themed poems I completed the same day and presented at the evening meal. During these modest postponements, Debbie's look of near imperceptible disappointment at breakfast never went unnoticed. Ne'er a word did she utter. Yet I knew that she knew I noticed.

One might correctly intuit my actions at the beginning of Debbie's diagnosis were more to satisfy *my need* to do something extra, not merely sit on the sidelines and provide a husband's perfunctory morale support. Not that I failed her during her first cancer treatments; of course, rendering loving understanding and moral support. I also naturally picked up most of the family chores, expected from one whose spouse entered the scary unknown of potentially long-term cancer treatments. Yet, these efforts focused more on physical tasks: cooking, shopping, cleaning, daily or weekly trips to the cancer center. The latter endeavor I never delegated to another soul. Nor did I miss a single treatment session over both therapy periods. But I was not convinced that I had left everything on the field. Some might opine I am being too hard on myself in thinking this way. Yet sometimes even when we believe we are giving every ounce of effort to a given situation, in retrospect we "Monday morning quarterback," and see other ways where improvements could be made.

This was all new for me as well, becoming caregiver for Debbie and her 96-year-old mom, Sweetie, an endearing family nickname, for the first time in 2015. But I did undergo a period of "caregiver-light" in assuming full legal responsibility for my father's sister from ages 87-94 while she resided in assisted living, selected by Debbie and me, many states away, beginning in the year 2001. Not the same by far, but the sense of accomplishment enhanced by the love and appreciation received from her stayed with me. I pictured my dad looking down at me with a much-surprised smile on his face. Exhausting, mentally and physically, emotionally draining are the best words to describe experiencing new challenges taking care of Debbie and her mom. At the same time extremely gratifying. Perhaps not unlike what many working mom's experience today. As time progressed, I got better at balancing all the demands and with Debbie's new treatments on the way, I wasn't beginning from scratch. In fact, I had retained some fondness, short of love, for cooking certain dishes. And in addition to preparing a hearty breakfast every day for all of us "breakfast people," I had acquired some degree of amateur cook status that served us well throughout our redefined daily regimen.

In 2015, cancer struck for the first time, breast cancer of the triple-negative variety, in Debbie's right breast. She opted for a lumpectomy that revealed a slight spreading to a "few" lymph nodes under her arm. Because of this, protocol called for chemotherapy, where radiation-only would normally have followed surgery. Triple negative made this cancer somewhat rare, (10%) with much lower survivability rate, 73% versus 93% with the common varieties. The rate lessened for recurrence. Protocol for less invasive varieties includes follow-on hormonal therapy, for life. Triple negative cancer cells lack the estrogen, and progesterone receptors (and HER2 protein) necessary for hormonal therapy to work. Everything appeared to go better than we expected, with the occasional bump in the road- a process consuming some nine months.

Just before Debbie's last scheduled chemotherapy session in a routine movement arising from our couch, her ankle turned in her shoe, she fell, shattering her ankle badly. I've never seen anyone with this level of pain, including twenty-six years of active military service. It was a significant emotional event. Emergency surgery ensued, installing two mental braces and eleven permanent screws. Two weeks later, now confined to a wheelchair because crutches interfered with her previous underarm surgery, she began eight weeks of twice-daily radiation. Hefting the thirty-five-pound wheelchair into and out of the trunk twice a day severely stressed the already chronically poor degenerative disk disease of my lower back. I reminded myself that any inconvenience I suffered paled with what her body and mind were enduring. These days were the toughest of the year on her, me and Sweetie. Incredulously, Debbie never complained nor asked "why me, Lord?" Throughout these trials, she never exhibited the mental or emotional distress most would expect to surface. Always the optimist, she simply trusted she would heal and the necessary steps bringing her back to normal would be taken. She trusted her team of surgeons, cancer specialists and faith in the Lord. We both did. And for a time, all did, in fact, return to normal. The year 2015 receded to the back of our minds, as if it never occurred. Our 2016 began and ended with multiple vacations including overseas. We thoroughly enjoyed ourselves. One of our best years for sure.

For the next two years we both rode the emotional high that comes from believing "we tamed this beast," even while the doctors had not proclaimed remission status. But her type of cancer possesses monstrous tentacles, rarer and more prone to rapid growth and recurrence, often rejoining imaging scans short of two years. This tidbit of information had not been previously revealed by the doctor. He, not more than we, expressed great satisfaction over this achievement, two years free. While not persuaded from thinking she was out of the woods, a surge of positive expectation swarmed over both of us, at this revelation. In fact, Debbie was convinced she had been completely cured, a healthy attitude for sure. I was less sanguine. The temporary euphoria lasted two more years before being gut-punched by an annual MRI, discovering the nasty savage had returned in the general area of the initial cancer. Her medical team decided this was not new but recurrent cancer. The radiologist said outright "we clearly did not get it all." One new fact we learned in this iteration revealed that current imaging technology as of this writing in 2021 falls short of detecting individual cancer cells. There must be a concentration of approximately one million cells for visual detection. A shocking epiphany. Even being in remission must be taken with a grain of salt.

After much consultation, soul searching and wrenching of hands, Debbie decided to undergo a bi-lateral mastectomy. The hardest decision rested not on this but on whether to embark on another round of chemotherapy, plus the normal radiation after surgery. She questioned the efficacy of the first chemo. In her mind, the first round clearly "did not work." Together with the substantial "chemo-brain" side-affects, why should she submit to another round? Ultimately, she chose to do so. The crowning argument posited by our two Physician Assistant children, Michael (47) and Jaime (43) and the loving me, centered on intangible points. She did get four years of freedom as this aggressive form of cancer often recurs as soon as two years. Perhaps, without the chemo, recurrence would have come sooner. You really cannot say the chemo did not work. There was no hard selling on these points, just soft-spoken logic of sorts. The decision was left entirely to her, as it should have been. She needed to be comfortable with the decision and the outcomes. We spent the better part of the next year, 2019, executing this even more aggressive chemo, with a slightly different and stronger mixture of the toxins.

Another decision not quite as difficult to make involved whether to opt for implants or for a complete reconstruction using tissue from other parts of her body. One wrinkle to this revolved around permanent or temporary breast implants during the surgery. This decision could not be made decisively beforehand, only a preference.

Permanent direct implants at the time of surgery required assessment of blood flow, conditions of remaining breast tissue and other factors. The benefits of direct implants swayed her in that direction and amazingly she qualified, and the plastic surgeon followed her breast surgeon in accomplishing that.

Yet, the final pathology report indicated that the margin between breast and muscle could not be confirmed as clear of cancer. We were told what every cancer patient dreads to hear: "we cannot say we got it all." After much consultation and some sleepless nights, we agreed with the doctor not to pursue further very invasive surgery into the pectoral muscle group. In the final analysis there is no certainty cancer will not reappear. Of course, that is always the case. No one offered guarantees at any step in the process. Our team, we thought, were professional, experts in their field, empathetic and kind throughout both cancer regimens. Both Debbie and I were and continue to be most grateful for this. Of course, routine follow-up testing and doctor visits continue for life.

I watched with amazement, appreciation and awe at the courage and resilience my sweetheart displayed throughout each of these horrific cancer treatment experiences. She never complained about any of it, including twice a day radiation during the twilight of the second round of treatments. During the period when my brother unexpectedly passed away, we both drove some seven hours to and from the funeral site out of state, returning just in time for her to make it to the cancer center for that's day's second dosing, having achieved the first before the trip at 6:00 AM. At this writing, we are a mere eighteen months removed from this trauma. And life is excellent.

To extract the most meaning from the poems that follow, a historical context of Debbie's and my relationship over fifty-nine years might prove enlightening, adding context. Many of the poems refer to some activities early in our relationship. Debbie and I became great friends in the eighth grade, after I successfully "encouraged" my parents to release me from seven years of local Catholic school, complete with nuns and priests. In a twist of serendipity, with last names beginning "ST" and "SW," our school lockers appeared side-by-side. And so, our long friendship began. At the time both of us were going "steady" with someone so there was no real opportunity to be anything but great friends, which we were.

Several of my poems highlight events such as chance encounters with Debbie even before this first official greeting. Little did I know that just a few months before meeting at school lockers she spotted me riding by on my bike in town. She thought I looked her age and wondered why we hadn't met in a town with only two schools. Soon she would know the answer. An interesting adjunct to this story involves a song the Australian pop group Savage Garden released as a huge hit in 1999 titled "I Knew I Loved You." The lyric that Debbie said captured her feeling about the chance sighting and subsequent relationship reads "I knew I loved you before I met you, I think I dreamed you into life." While this might seem a bit too fairy-tale-ish to be remotely true, this is her vision of the emotion she felt way back then, as described to me. She really, really loves this song.

Free of our "steadies," we dated briefly in the ninth grade. After three months, Debbie broke up with me. She claimed I was not the same as when we were merely best friends, a time during which we might chat for hours about really nothing. I was shocked. Astonishingly, our friendship remained strong. Then in the summer before our tenth grade, my tennis coach, Bill Riordan (later Jimmy Connor's business manager) arranged for me to spend a year in Florida where the weather allowed year-round playing. I spent a full year away from home living with four different families in south Florida. There, I completed against some of the nation's best in the off-season. In a perfect world, success defined at the time would produce a lofty Florida state ranking, a coveted prize contributing to elevated seeding in the next summer's national tournament circuit. In fact, I was amazingly successful and would have achieved the stated goal. My game did improve, I improved my national ranking to 13 and added State and Middle Atlantic regional championships to five each before high school graduation. These achievements led directly to multiple full and partial collegiate scholarship. I give full credit to Bill Riordan who set all of this up. Unfortunately, for reasons I never discovered he pulled back as my coach before my year in Florida ended. I played my last two years without a coach or tennis mentor.

As I ended my 10th grade there, the Florida Tennis Association informed me that I was not eligible for a state ranking, due to my shortened residence, clearly reneging on its original promise. I suspect the parents of some of my opponents rose up in protest. The experience, bereft of female companionship, excessive loneliness, mission failure of sorts since I definitely improved, and a feeling of general malaise, left me desperately wanting to secure the steadying relationship with a hometown girl upon my return.

As I returned from Florida at the end of the school year my best friend at the time, whom I recently lost to pancreatic cancer, Dan, arranged a double date for us. He suggested a girl other than Debbie, but his "steady," one of Debbie's best friends, even to this day, intervened. Debbie became my date. And so, on September 5th, 1965 – a date still meaningful so many years later, our real journey

11

began. I know, you expected me to say, "a day that will live in infamy." Catchy phase just seems a little over the top. We remained "steady" in our friendship that grew into the deep satisfying love we share today. Of course, there were challenges along the way, like attending college in different states. I, at West Point, which allowed no "off campus" (really an Army base) freedom for the first three years; she, at the University of Maryland. Yet, we persevered through high school and college. Debbie went out of her way to visit me at West Point, suffering long smelly bus rides and overnighting in a girl's dormitory established outside the West Point gate for visiting girls. And spending what little money she had from a small allowance allocated by her mom and dad. In fact, I know she often went without just to save money to visit me. I took that for granted. Just add that to the growing list of my sins of omission.

I would be remiss, dishonest even by omission, not mentioning my ill-factored (may the good Lord forgive me) feeble attempt to break up with Debbie once at sixteen citing my dad's advice to not get tied down to one girl, but to "date around." Later, I discovered Dad's real concern: he dated a young lady steadily for seven years and never married. Fortunately, I failed in my wretched break-up attempt. Clearly one of my life's most potentially singular failures turned miracle. Debbie astutely argued that boys in our little town of Salisbury, Maryland did not "date around." With skillful logic she slowly articulated that every one of our friends became coupled, going "steady," a term used in those days. She argued that if not with her, I would likely be going steady with one of her friends. Clearly not satisfactory by her reasoning. That being the case, she contended "you may as well be with me, then, as you certainly will not be 'dating' the field, and most definitely not my friends." I remember clearly that night, parked in Dad's car in our secret place, where we frequently went to be alone and, you know, "talk." I remained quiet for some time, considering her point, seeking internal wisdom, counterpoints-holes in her logic. I came up empty. Praying for guidance failed. I caved. Nevermore did I entertain this insane notion. Debbie clearly was leaving nothing to chance. She left everything on the field. And it worked, thankfully.

With other mistakes along the way by my reckoning, I still had much to make up for. Oh, nothing like infidelity, inattention or bereft of intense love, as I was, am now and will forever be simply a "one women man." Thinking back on this time of my life, there is no doubt in my mind that events leading to our improbable union, rife with roadblocks, could only have occurred with seeds planted in both of us by the Lord, God. Hallelujah!

We married three days after I graduated West Point and donned my Army uniform for at least the next five years, a legal commitment. Many (ok all) of my close friends who knew Debbie well due to her frequent visits to West Point over four years, claimed then and still strongly maintain "Jack, you definitely married up." I have never disputed this. Unlike many wives in those Vietnam days of the early seventies, Debbie took to military life as geese to a golf course. Posted initially in Germany, then to Italy I "enjoyed" as much as five days a week away from home in field training. Our Army strategy at the time centered on a European presence established after World War II to deter Russian aggression and assure our allies of overt physical support. Debbie learned quickly to make friends and became an integral part of the military family, a trait that served both of us well throughout my twenty-six-year active-duty career. In all, by informal calculation I determined I'd spent at least five years away from her and later our two children during those years. Veterans refer to separation as one of the "X" factors of military life that requires special strength of character qualities for a family to endure. We knew many that were unable to adjust and cope with a life so different from ordinary civilian experiences. Throughout all of this Debbie remained steadfastly by my side. She embodied the ethos of a true partner in a sometimes-otherworldly journey, loving me, encouraging me, advising me and then raising our two wonderful children. Without her, those early years might very well have gone awry.

In 1990, my eighteenth year of Army service, I deployed to southwest Asia as a battalion commander with nearly 1,000 troops (swelling to nearly 3,000) under my command. Troops from Iraq had invaded nearby Kuwait, ostensibly to control the country's oil supplies. The Army named this "conflict" Desert Storm and deployed massive warfighter and logistic support to challenge this attack on the sovereignty of Kuwait. As was and still is the Army's practice, the wife of a commander deployed with troops took charge of an activity aptly named the Family Support Group (FSG). This Group comprised the wives of all subordinate commanders' as well as the wives of the battalion's senior non-commissioned officers. Their mission concentrated on providing all necessary support to the nearly 700 wives of my battalion who remained at home, in some instances as young as sixteen. In many cases a young spouse remained at home woefully unprepared to fend for themselves. Additionally, a number of Soldiers were single parents and petitioned other extended family take over the responsibilities for one or more children. After a long deployment, occasionally this "responsible person" decided the chore exceeded their ability or desire to remain the surrogate parent. Imagine a deployed Soldier receiving news of this.

My problems overseas paled in comparison to some of the personal situations Debbie found herself forced to handle. At least I was trained to handle most of issues I encountered. Debbie was not. On occasion, I would get a message from my chain of command to call Debbie. She would uncover problems that in very few instances required immediate decisions by me to send a Soldier home. Without her personal knowledge and involvement, I never would have known that one of my Soldiers had such severe problems at home that likely would inhibit full attention on our important mission. Understand that telephone service was available to troops even in the desert, courtesy of AT&T. And the troops communicated somewhat frequently with their family members.

One case I recall involved one of my Soldiers calling home to be met with an unknown male voice. This person was now living with my Soldier's wife. While not common, word of these breaches spread like wildfire through the unit. Other Soldiers imagined this might happen to them. In consultation with a Soldier's chain of command, I made decisions to send a few home. Upon return to Ft. Bragg months later, one wife came up to me with tears in her eyes. She profoundly thanked me for sending her husband home. "It saved my marriage" she claimed. Of course, a deployed force in a combat zone could not complete its mission if scores of Soldiers were sent home. It was a rare occurrence and my recommendation had to be cleared way up my chain of command.

You can see how important Debbie's role became to those at home station (Ft. Bragg, N.C.) and well as to the deployed under my command. There were many more less severe issues that Debbie solved without me ever knowing. Imagine the weight she took on, voluntarily, in addition to caring for two teenagers. I was and am still in awe of her when I think back on those time. Another accumulated debt.

For Soldiers deployed to hostile areas of operations, especially for unknown periods of time, their focus must be on the task at hand. Mission success demands their full attention. Distractions at home, the possibilities of which seemed endless, could result in a serious loss of focus, and ultimately might cost the lives of some wonderful men and women. So, the FSG was not just a name given to a group of women with a hallow mission. Severe issues arose requiring real and immediate action. For me, Debbie and the Group she led were important unsung heroes of Desert Storm beginning in 1990 and ending well into the next year. Not many, if any, books were written about these wonderful unpaid volunteers, unfortunately. Added to what I considered an overdue debt, I couldn't compensate my resplendent wife for having to take on this essential volunteer responsibility. Neither did the Army.

As with all other aspects of expected spousal "duties" Army wives withstood, Debbie willingly and proactively assumed the role the Lord prepared for her. All the while, in spectacular fashion, she continued raising my two amazing teenage children. How could I not seek ways to elevate her to the quintessential position of ultimate love and respect. I owed her that and more. I still do. Some debts, real or imagined can never be fully repaid. As a footnote to this story, word of the success of the new program reached Pentagon levels. Representatives were dispatched to see and learn the backstories leading to the positive outcomes. I discovered that her leadership and management processes became the gold standard for operating Family Support Groups army wide. I just described Debbie's version of *leaving it all on the field*. I couldn't have been prouder.

Returning home from eight months in the desert, we shopped for a full-size replacement to the large Oldsmobile station wagon that broke down soon after my deployment. Our second car had filled in until my return, as the cost of repair could not be justified against the car's age. Unimaginably, we filled the void with a shiny new 1991 red Mazda Miata (sportscar) in lieu of the practical family car. While out looking for a boring station wagon replacement, Debbie mentioned "I really would like a red convertible sports car to drive before my hair turns grey." I listened. The Miata was a fairly new model on the market, hard to find and not readily discounted. I offered a "deal" to several local car dealers, who basically laughed at my request to pay $300 over their cost for the highly prized car. With a philosophy that served me well into the future, I knew I needed to find only one dealer to agree. Using the yellow pages, I called every dealer within fifty miles and found my one. He said in selling the car "let this be a well-deserved coming home present for you and your wife." I voted to canonize him a saint immediately. That car still has a place in our garage, looking as good as the day we rode it home, thirty years later. At least on this occasion, I think I left it all on the field.

Returning to the recent past. The joy in Debbie's face and voice as she read each poem aloud, then shared with Sweetie, could only have been met with an equal or even greater elation on my part. My purpose in bringing joy, love and unconditional support to her was being fulfilled. This gift to her filled my emotional glass to the brim. The daily cathartic sense of purpose energized my soul and physical well-being to an incalculable high, thus empowering me to accomplish all I needed to without faltering too much. My chicken casseroles even improved. Of course, I had moments of darkness involuntarily creeping into the crevices of my sub-conscious. You will see some, but not all, of the poems I composed during those moments of doubt and melancholy. I aptly named my computer file with these poems "My Dark Moments." Naturally, I did not share these with Debbie during moments of weakness or at all. Later in Debbie's treatment cycle, the darkness and fear in me grew less murky. The fog of fear lessoned, and I began to write more uplifting verse that still remained private. Since I was still cranking out my daily verses for Debbie, I saw no need to share these at the time, nor later, until now. She will see my dark poems and the lighter verses for the first time in Part II of this book. Am I nervous about that? You bet. Composing poems and presenting them in a daily private setting is one thing. But, to share intimate thoughts and emotions with potentially complete strangers in book form is quite another. In fact it terrifies me.

There are many reasons I undertook to publish this book. Chief among them falls directly to my passion of offering "public" tribute of a documented nature to the most genuine, lovable and beautiful person with whom I've been best friends since we were thirteen. I want my current extended family and future generations to know our story, hopefully learning something from it as well as my version of *leaving it all on the field*. In my world, the English language simply doesn't contain enough breathtaking adjectives to convey my deepest admiration and appreciation of God's gift to me. Debbie would say "our gift to one another." From her I learned how to open my heart for unconditional love. I survived the adolescent passion engendered by raging hormones, parental divorce while we dated, college separation and the unsavory emotional baggage-producing relationship with my father which affected my relationship with Debbie for years before and into marriage. To celebrate all of these gifts, I unveiled my gratitude to Debbie with this book on our fiftieth anniversary in June of 2021, after twenty-four months in the making.

Another goal in sharing these poems reflects a desire to highlight the potential effect and toll on spouses who by necessity become caregivers. Thrust suddenly into this role for which one is untrained and unprepared, a plethora of elevated emotions, displayed visibly or kept internally, will most assuredly influence attitudes and sentiments. These in turn, are absorbed by the very person you have vowed to protect against such emotional transgressions. In my case, these dark moments seemed to arise most frequently as I sat watching Debbie sleeping while undergoing her chemo regimen. In my limited research, I found this reaction not unusual, and believe I kept these rueful moments for the most part private, sharing any negative emotions with my pen and paper, rather with Debbie. Not that I would have, but also there were no animals to kick. Guilty feelings nearly always accompanied these times. Guilt because I knew very well the current suffering was not about me. My sole reason for being centered on staying focused, positive and lovingly supportive of Debbie. Yet, the subconscious doesn't always align one's intent nor logic. Involuntary melancholy sometimes consumes our spirit despite diametric motives. I won't claim perfection in hiding my angst. Yet the spiritual release gained through daily writing, investing myself, extending myself toward Debbie, played a major role in suppressing a sometimes-negative psyche.

Next, this book represents my attempt to demonstrate to myself, friends, family and any others who may find themselves in the same position as Debbie and me that travelling the extra mile is worthy of the effort. It's more than okay to "leave it all on the field;" to exhibit seemingly strange or unique forms of support and encouragement and to struggle with the weight of frustration, disappointment and even depression. By sharing my ups and downs in the form of poems, I hope my convergence to the positive side of my nature may help others in similar situations understand and perhaps better cope with their challenges, as I was able to do, eventually. The *force* (of the Lord) was truly with me.

While I believe I am and have been a good, loving and faithful husband, I realized I had not left everything *on the field of marriage.* Amidst the times of great trial in both instances of Debbie's cancer, the light came on in blazing fashion. I examined both my private and public demonstrability of love, respect and admiration for my best friend in life. The motivation and desire to exalt her to the well-deserved and revered place already in my heart and soul but lacking somewhat in the physical world came into focus. As the expression goes "I was and still am a work in progress," as a fledgling wannabe poet, husband and father. My Academy roommate, best man at my wedding, and an accomplished amateur poet and writer himself, upon reading a few of my earlier poems for Debbie, commented "you have some potential, Jack." Afterwards, I had to laugh to myself. I wondered if I reached the ripe old age of 95, would I live long enough to fulfill this potential. I think not. As this book will be my only publication, a positive outcome to fulfilling any potential is less than certain.

My intent then is to show that writing poetry, giving daily cards of love and encouragement, whispering sweet somethings are all part and parcel of "leaving it all on the field." We men all, hopefully, gift our wives with the obligatory flowers, candy, jewelry along our journey of marriage. Many do much more. Yet, I discovered way too late in life that presenting one rose or two dozen roses on a special occasion evoked much the same response. It's not the size of the gift, but the thought, effort, timing and ingenuity of the gift that makes all the difference in the response. (See "Is One Rose Too Many?") The "little girl inside" smile and love I saw every day in Debbie reading my poems filled me and apparently her with such joy. A thousand roses delivered in one bunch could never have evinced the same reaction. It was magical for me. And I believe Debbie became even more positive and uplifted that her normal mien gave expression to.

The message to myself and others is simple: leave nothing undone when it comes to honoring your significant other. One cannot dispense enough love, respect and admiration. You simply cannot overdo it. God's cup overflows with these elements. Never worry the well will run dry. If you think it, do it or express it. If you believe "this just isn't me," think again; try harder. Never put yourself in a position that on your death bed you ponder, *I wish I had done more to demonstrate how I really feel about...* Some might call writing poetry leaving it all on the field, or conversely *a distortion in the force*, crazy, or an aberration. I would say leaving something of my heart and soul on the field to join my team of two, doubles the chance for a long-term union of joy and happiness, that otherwise might be elusive.

The entire experience revolved around maintaining a home environment as normal as possible, being a caring caregiver, a purveyor of inspiration, encouragement, love, support and "day laborer" as required (thanks for the label, Jerry). The inculcation of all this coalesces in this book, and for me, defines "leaving all of myself on the field." Since my forte' in sports fell in the world of tennis, I could substitute "court" for "field," albeit with much less impact. Where you leave "it" isn't as essential as simply leaving it. Decide how and when it's most impactful to your significant other. Poetry helped me achieve that. What would you substitute for poetry? What is your poetry? What and where is your field of consequence?

I admit that some of my friends, even close friends, have poked fun at some of my "fielding plays." In a rare instance I posted a poem on Facebook. Probably for birthday or anniversary. More than one said, "why Facebook, couldn't you just have kept it private? You're making the rest of us look bad." Yes, of course, was the answer. Yet, if one of my silent friends, even one, becomes inspired to lay him or herself open and vulnerable to such jesting, after reading of my experience here and takes action to "leave their 'it' all on the field" in whatever relationship appropriate to their life, then I will have met another of my goals in completing this book. And please don't forget my portion of the royalty check if your successful effort goes viral. Kidding of course.

Finally, you will see some variety of scenarios I chose to convey my messages to Debbie. I certainly wondered how many ways I might discover to say, "I love you, I admire your strength and courage, I am with you all the way, etc." I found this less difficult than expected, occasionally mixing in some humor and references to our early lives before marrying. There are even selections on French Toast and Ribs. You must continue reading to discover the context. Spoiler: there are no secret family recipes divulged. Sometimes, not focusing on "the issue," injecting humor, became a positive force for the day.

For those that may find themselves in our position, I heartily encourage an approach that leaves both you and your loved one in a better place, day to day. No one except you or others that have experienced and lived through the rigors of a loved one's cancer horror, simultaneously with caregiving, can truly understand. There are nearly always at least some other lives directly affected, even if one lives alone. I offer to anyone who finds a poem here they just love (hopefully at least one) to copy and paste it into your own card. Make the day for your significant other. Their reaction will also make your day. It's the least he or she deserves.

In light of the unanticipated length of this Introduction, for those already saturated with words, please feel free to thumb through the images. Poetry is not for everyone; my hope is that my "pictures" stimulate your imagination. I designed each one to stimulate creative juices and give visual context to the poetic words accompanying them.

PART I

The following poems were written, typed and pasted inside a card then presented to Debbie daily at breakfast during her chemotherapy and radiation protocols.

.

Getting Back Up

Here's the important thing about life:
It deals with love, relationships and strife.
We get kicked in the shins, too oft to count.
Yet we never permanently dismount.
Watching You fight, with all Your might
Inspires us all to avoid the fright
That knocks on our door without warning,
But lifts us on our horse every morning.

Those who know Debbie well will know this image is not based in reality. In fact, she has always been reluctant to get very near horses, claiming "they are so huge, especially the head." But the metaphor of the poem was too true to resist this illustration, even though in real life fainting comes to mind.

Share Your Burden

Hanging in there means hanging out HERE
Staying close to "us," staying near.

Let Us share the weight on your shoulders
Allow Us to help heave these boulders.

Let Him shatter the burden with love
Freely dispensed from the Lord above.

Walk with Him through this scorching fire;
Squelch the pain, seek the ground that's higher.

Rely not only on your best defenses
As the great battle for life commences.

I am part of your harmonious choir,
Lean on me too; being your rock is my desire.

"Bear one another's burdens, and so fulfill the law of Christ." Galatians 6:2

Cloaked in Love

I sit and watch you from my ridged chair
Preparing for the meds we cannot share.
A little nervous but you don't show it
Would rather be having a banana split.

You're all bundled up in a gifted throw,
As our chatty nurse prepares the ammo.
Beginning with meds they call pre-treating
I notice your wakefulness is fleeting.

Wanting to wrap myself around you then
Dispensing comfort again and again.
The minutes seemed to drag ever so slowly
But we're committed to all of this wholly.

It's over now, and we must go
Healing has begun, as we both know.
I'm so proud of everything you are
My beautiful rose and shiny bright star.

Dainty Headwraps

I pray as I watch you silently sleep
That my darling may always keep
Smiling throughout the treatments we seek –
To crush malevolence into the deep
Chasms of time never to repeat.
You look so perky in dainty headwraps.
'Specially with recent symptoms' collapse,
Now for a fortnight you can just relax.
Thankful that harsher effects did elapse,
And you were mostly spared those awful craps.

Internal Resilience

We know the expression "hang in there,"
Meant to inspire unrelenting strength
In the face of grim threats that doth ensnare.
Then we ask, will peace come at length?
There is no weakness in thus abiding
If merely by our fingertips we do cling.
Knowing our weary steps God is guiding
To a path of healing only He can bring.
My darling's grip is most secured
Extending beyond token resistance
Into a space where she'll not be ignored,
Celestial light will propel her the distance.
While hope is essential, a key role to play
Hope without strength is an empty choice.
There must be more for our ailing to allay
And my sweetheart's got it, on that I rejoice.

God's Wing Unfurled

It is true you're living a dream
Of challenges outside of extreme?
When others ne'er fail to scream
You gather a positive head of steam.
Enlarging your magnetic allure
Creating images that forever endure,
And virtues no one can ignore –
Craving your moral fiber to secure.
Seeking strength doesn't work
'Cause innate weakness may lurk.
You've received the Lord's perk
To reject the negative earthwork
That infests our everyday world
With impatience and anger unfurled.
As you navigate the cancer hurled
While under God's wing you stay curled.

"He shall cover you with His feathers, and under His wings you Shall take refuge; His truth shall be your shield and buckler" Psalm 91-4

Tired Days

I really hate when your tail's not waggin'
Cause you feel tired and are a draggin'
Your lips ain't movin' your eyelids are saggin'
Add to this, too many folks naggin'
At least on my cookin' yur not gaggin'
Here's hopin' yur tail's soon awaggin'

Miss Optimism

You are a metaphor for sunny thoughts
Absorbing rays, only positives sought.
Sunshine today means joy tomorrow
Storing today's joy for later to borrow.
No angst allowed to penetrate your peace

How Am I Chosen?

The Beauty of your mien evinces strength
Of mind, body and soul melding at length.
We tackle setbacks to our wellbeing
Attuned to these virtues that define us
And protecting those most prodigious,
Endowed by the divine Supreme Being.

Some illnesses make us silently weep
With stamina challenged daily to keep.
Pain and suffering of treatments vary
Perseverance dictates various response.
Some patients feign elusive nonchalance
While doctor's advice lurks cautionary.

Is it merely fate that chooses its prey,
Pulling a number as if witches play?
Are some beyond vulnerable fair game?
The kind and meek seem unfairly exposed
And the gentle even more so disposed,
This inequity is a crying shame.

It's troublesome not to thanklessly muse
My sweetheart couldn't her cancer refuse.
A journey echoed from four years ago
Recovery seeing a vile turn around,
As cancer again into her was ground
We pray an angel will help vanquish this foe.

Glass Half Full

What meaning lies in the phrase "glass half full?"
Do we know of our natural leaning?
Does the devil in opposition pull?
Will "Fullness" give life more truthful meaning?

A joy in life is one's predilection
From this penchant our psyche permits
A "glass half full" to see this direction
And fill the space with decanter's French-kiss.

My Love's compelling unquenchable thirst
Must fill the glass and maintain it just so,
Avoiding emptiness and it's accursed
Ejecting hostile cargo from depths below.

The taste of your breath does indeed reflect
A lifetime of drinking only the best –
And nectars of sweetness that you collect
Releasing them sweetly to all you've blessed.

A lifetime of moxie filled to the brim,
Purest vintage; fine wine to the senses.
This cup of spirits sates every limb
As optimism conquers all defenses.

Chutzpah Galore

You gotta be tough to handle cancer
Singer, writer or belly dancer
Might lack the moxie to survive;
Must be a mom with kids to thrive.

Ability to make hard decisions
Sometimes compromising on visions –
Raising kids who refuse to listen
Has one ever gone missin'?

Enduring the pain of childbirth
Living nine months with a colossal girth.
Using survival skills invented on the fly
As necessary, ululating a battle cry.

These are traits that typify tough
Ensuring you are always brave enough
To face adversities while remaining calm,
That's what it takes to be a good mom.

Combining virtues required to endure
With strength and bravery will come the cure,
My sweetheart is more than just a mother
She has the chutzpah this cancer to smother.

"You will never do anything in this world without courage. It is the greatest quality of the mind next to honor." Aristotle

---

Awesome Together

Together we are awe-inspirin'
Single minded without perspirin.'
In crisis there can be no "me"
Neither of us can thrive alone.
Jointly we face the dark unknown
Hand in hand marching inexorably.

With our union never faltering
Our hearts paired unaltering
Beating in-step with the notion:
Happy and together, in balance.
For each other we make allowance
Synched as one with our devotion.

Lifeline

While a rising tide lifts all boats,
What if you lack such conveyance?
Overboard without any hopes
And your life's held in abeyance

Some are always left in the water
Overboard grasping for invisible ropes,
Before they choke on saltwater
Will anyone help rescue the folks?

The parallel to life warns us
To live each day as if it's our last,
Guarding the lifeline to all that's precious
Coping today, ignoring our past.

You darling, hold the key to my soul
Unlocking what makes me vulnerable
So, we both can assault it as whole.
Weaving the lifeline that's unassailable.

It's too hard to achieve this alone
Unknowingly you sense my concern –
As if it were carved in stone
My lifeline, expecting nothing in return.

How Ironic. I wanted to ease her pain, assuage her anxiety...Uplift HER; be HER lifeline. And yet, I think the opposite occurred. A serendipitous by-product. And oh, the stress of the moment played with my vision a bit, cause we all know Debbie is not blond.

A Worthy "Poop"

This poop shall pass,
It was not meant to last.
And there are benefits too,
It's not all useless goo.
*The nutrients it may bring
Especially during each Spring
Leave grass much greener
Lifting our demeanor.
*And think of all the flowers
Adding verve to their powers
And what we love the most:
Our roses on which we can boast.

Forever Love

Our love can do anything.
In fact, it has done everything:
Lubricated our emotional core,
Coupled our souls as never before,
~~Without ensuring we never snore~~
Blissfully enchanted us ever more,
Prepared for our after-life encore,
Lifted our hearts to evermore soar,
Served up a model no one could ignore,
And opened to us Heavenly gate's door.

Hairballs in Life

In the hairball scheme of life
There's too much suffering and strife.

It sticks in our crawl, refusing to leave
In surrender, to it we cleave.

Yet some like the cat are able to hack,
Or as you, denying what makes others crack.

Discharging the scraps of leftover angst
We're liberated and to the Lord give thanks.

Unflappable with peace in your being,
Absorbing all that supports well-being…

It's the secret sauce of hanging on
And the recipe for making you strong.

Pull Yourself Up

The canyon looms, the current rages fierce
Suspended high with chaos nipping heels,
You thought this scourge could ne'er the body pierce
Yet turmoil roils as deep persuasion heals.

As though bewitched your body hauls the load,
Essential calm must rule expected surge
Of emotions stored today, and later bestowed;
Engender strength, combined with heart to merge.

Act now surrender nil, look up, force hands
In tandem seizing hope to seal the grate
Or fall, becoming compost for the lands.
Being swept by raging currents and fate!

Remain untouchable, unbreakable
Escape the pain, the devil, the evil
Of ghostly wraiths, posing unmistakable.
Destroy their power, derail the sequel.

Reach up, keeper of my heart and soul
Though weary, heat the marrow of thy bones,
Escape now, grab hold of what you control:
As faith restores the mind and bodies it owns.

We'll Have the Toast

We have waffles, we can have pancakes,
But I draw the line having them with milkshakes.
We love our eggs, sausage and crispy bacon
But why oh why have we French toast forsaken.

The work is hard, ingredients complex,
We know the reward of what comes next.
My vow to you as we march into Fall:
Enrich our menu to the glee of all.

I've been thrifty: goodies once a week,
You don't complain, refusing to shriek –
I'm sorry and promise to do better
I won't get to heaven as a chintzy debtor.

We have always enjoyed a full breakfast: eggs, meat, fruit, pancakes, sweets,
etc. Since Debbie's first cancer in 2015, when I took over all cooking chores,
breakfast remained "full." Yet, I never tried to duplicate Debbie's special recipe
for French Toast. Here I promise to change that. No pressure!

Internal Smiles

No chasm in time, nor realistic life
Ever makes you focus on strife.
No kick in the pants, can rip you asunder
Push you over the edge, pull you under.
Internal smiles keep you grounded here,
They also keep away all of the fear
That threatens to hold one down,
Interfering with the sought-after rebound.
Your inner strength and precious smile
Never fails to enrich your lifestyle.
And spread like wildfire over the land
Touching those as part of the Lord's plan.
It cannot be stopped this miracle of yours
Coming full circle to you in magical cures.

"You have power over your mind, not outside events. Realize this, and you will find strength." Marcus Aurelius

Our Trophy

I'm walking with you without stopping or pause
With no one beside us to clap nor applause,
Together for life no matter the distance
Lending my soul and its passion assistance

The road is long, bestowed with hidden potholes,
Hand in hand, we pursue what the next block holds.
One step, one block, into the traffic of life;
My darling, my sweetheart, my savior my wife.

There're no impediments we can't overcome
Combining our power not to succumb.
I see the prize at the end of our journey:
A doubles trophy for winning the tourney.

Blessed

I'm blessed for the kindness you reveal
Displayed infinitely in time
In the aura of your appeal –
A trait that cedes the most sublime.

The unmatched bouquet of your scale
Dispensed with rosy sweetness scent,
Persists throughout as you prevail
With God's grace from whom all is sent.

"The simple acts of kindness are by far more powerful than a thousand heads bowed in prayer." Mahatma Gandhi

---

Radiant Flux

The softness of your hands remain
Tho' cobbled with knobby joint pain
Flitting at the edges of your mind
Cocooned in defiance of relief declined.

The touch of your skin still heralds hope
As we utterly avoid the slippery slope
When scintillating light from our senses erupts
Charging our hands with a radiant flux.

Our World

I love you more than ever
Our bond will never sever
We will be joined forever
Our purpose engenders pleasure.
Our world was destined to be...
The way of our world you spin
Let's us both have cause to win
'Splains why we never give in
Forces us to get out or stay in.
Our world is God's gratuity...
Serenity without that fear
Is why we both stay near
Allowing none to interfere
For us there is no veneer.
Our world brings us security...
Caressed in the arms of trust
Always able to adjust
No thinking of dust to dust
Believe Heaven will be just.
YOU ARE THE WORLD TO ME!!!

Reborn

I gently rub the fuzz on your head
Unable to conceive the anguish,
Irreverently bestowed to you instead –
Yet, you simply refuse to languish.

The Lord comes to those of strong faith.
HE won't fail to carry you through.
It's in the words HE saithe
As you through HIM are born anew

From *Footprints in the Sand* poem (authorship disputed) The Lord replied "My precious child. I love you, and I would never, never leave you during your time of trial and suffering. When you saw only one set of footprints, It was then that I carried you." https://en.wikipedia.org/wiki/Footprints_(poem)

Dreamland

I lay my head on your torso
And feel the touch of your soft hand.
Stroking my head, and cheeks below
As I drift off into dreamland,
Feeling your love with ev'ry touch –
Preventing angst from taking hold.
My flesh sighs, but not overmuch,
As your hand does my core enfold.
Calming behavior ends each day.
As we seek to heal any bruises
That might have crept up, during the day.
Your tummy has so many great uses.

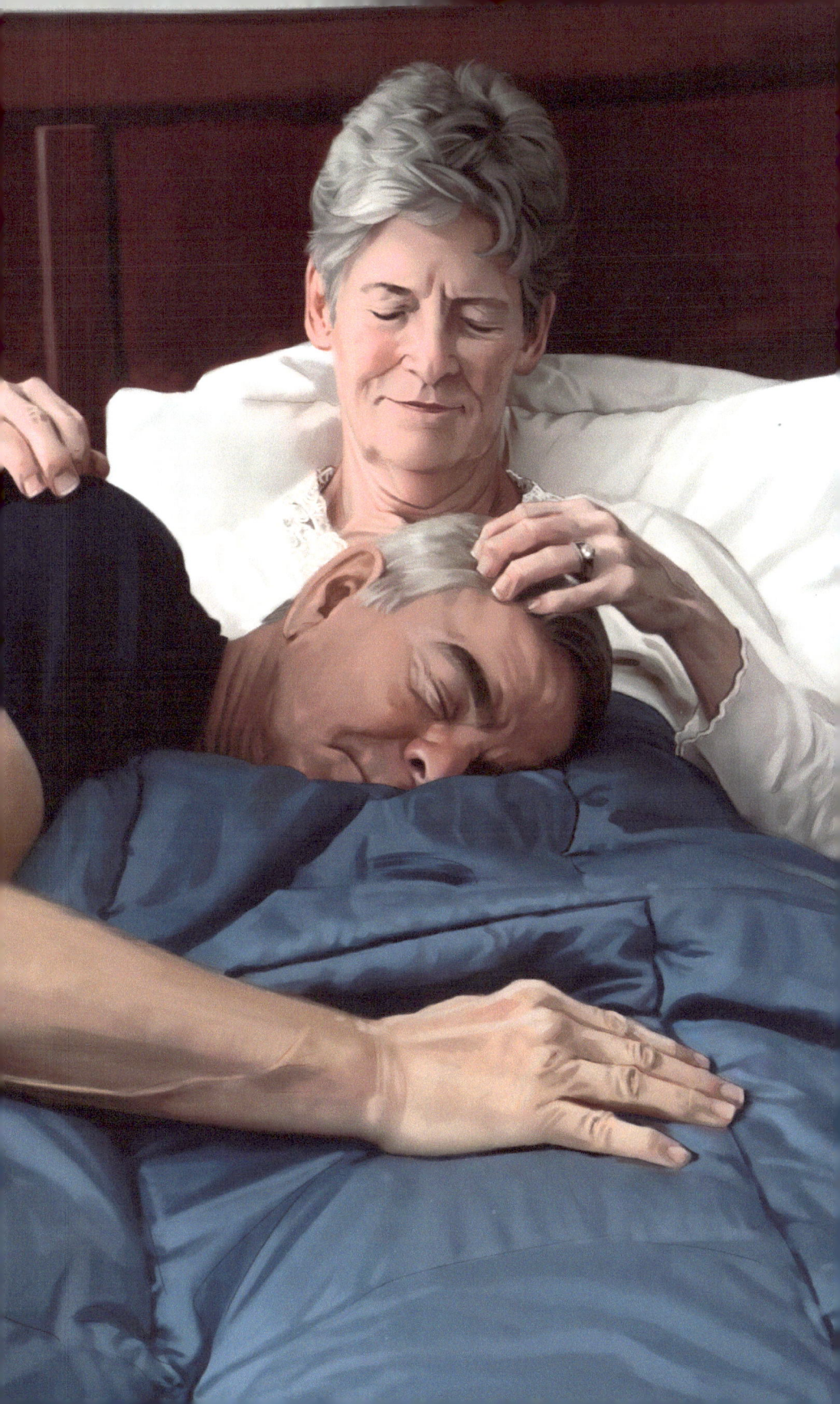

Joy Reigns

There is no Why in your demeanor
Nor thoughts of unfairness on which to dwell,
The grass on "the other side" is greener;
That your heaven has turned into fiery hell.

All you see is ample opportunity
Forging inexorably ahead
Refusing cancer's impunity
Tearing the disease to shreds.

There are no cries for "Why or Unjust;"
Crying in the night or seeing the worst.
Over you a sprinkle of angel dust
Scatters joy in which you're immersed.

The Power of Magic

Even when you are feeling unwell,
You are still subject to a perky spell.
So, hocus pocus, alakazam,
I declare you well, hot damn!
The magical words used for the hat
Work fine right now, much faster than that.
No sorcery needed, Your magic's intact
It's an obvious fact so don't clean up your act.
There's no power on this lovely earth
Strong 'nuff to dispatch intrinsic mirth.
Embedded so deep within the soul
So fertile and ripe defining Your whole.
What valued attribute might one render
To capture superpowers sans self-surrender.
The aura of magic that guides your joy
Is something time cannot destroy.
Just look to the heavens, enjoy the weather,
With me and Sweetie all together.

Life Can Be A 'Beach'

Many are the things I love about her:
Eschewing darkness others incur
Fixated only on the good in life
Avoiding all that is filled with strife.

Explaining what the rest cannot see
Living just now's best reality,
Recharging life's cup to the very brim
Disdaining everything dark and grim.

Consuming the nectar, wearing sensors
Detecting angst and pain she censors.
Reducing fears to lighthearted care
Showcasing how to give-up despair.

Comingling joy and love as covenants
Eliminating couldn't and cant's.
Determining spiritual ethos
Projecting perfectly poised pathos.

Pursuing moments of purest love
Engraining traits She's emblematic of,
Acquiring winsomeness of a mourning dove
Attiring God's love like a fitted glove.

She taught me the serene solution:
To the beach make a contribution,
Lay back, imbibe the beauty sublime
Leave chaos home for another time.

Our opposites DO attract. I am still a work in progress learning the serene from Debbie. If we could choose our favorite place to simply "be," this would be it. Serenity at its best. Notice the girlie drink for her and gin/tonic for me. And you didn't miss the Dunkin' Donuts box under the table. While life can be a "b___ch"; let's fill the half-empty glass with our own version of THE BEACH!!

The Dangerous Bear

Surely you know the danger of a bear
Purveyor of more than one can bear.
While it goes without saying
You must avoid slaying.
So do as you must to endure,
Even as sometimes you are not sure –
Don't hang in there just to hang
Into this challenge deeply sink your fang.

This grizzly is a pretty good replica of the bear that our daughter Jaime and family of four viewed while camping in Alaska where they live. Sitting one evening around the fire, this humongous head popped up nearby...and my oh my did they dash, all to their small camper. Fortunately, Yogi scampered away. And yes, they were stronger for the experience, at least practicing their bear-sighting plan.

WHAT doesn't
KILL you
makes you
STRONGER
except bears
BECAUSE
bears will
KILL YOU

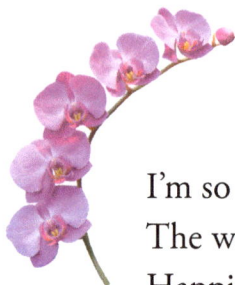

Simple Joy

I'm so glad I have you
The world is joyful too,
Happiness is in your smile
Radiance always your style.
No elusive veil to hide
Taking everything in stride
My alluring loving wife
And precious elixir of life.
How could one ever know
Which way the winds would blow?
As circling cranes seek prey aground
Then striking out unleashed, unbound
We too emerged to wander
Explore ourselves, futures to ponder.
In search of life's most precious gifts
We found the secret beyond the myths
Inside the blooming girl and boy
Love only spawns a life of simple joy.

God Answers

Prayer unites you to your soul
When the precipice bids you fall.
It won't allow your courage to pall,
Appending the soul to the celestial pole.

Each prayer emits its own intensity
To mimic passions of the sender.
Prayers of many doth music engender
As God listens with ascendency.

And so it is that your chain of prayer
Surging upward with such passion,
Scaling, swelling with much compassion
Is being heard, as He did declare.

"Whenever two or more are gathered together in my name, there am I in their midst." (Matthew 18:20)

One Step, One Day

One step at a time, one day at a time.
A model ingrained in your DNA.
Advancing you beyond all hills you climb,
Defeating challenges coming your way

How will you triumph outwitting this threat?
Batten the hatches, slowly tread ahead,
You're doing this now, sans breaking a sweat –
Averting negatives, leaving them unsaid.

The positive spin you hurl upon life
Defines best practices for all to learn.
As living in the moment for you is rife,
May your days bring forward all that you yearn.

Pure Enchantment

I'm so happy we have each other,
To love, snuggle and sometimes smother,
With kisses, holding hands and quiet affection
Simply to emphasize our amazing connection.

You and I, moored in a rapturous place
Fitting together in a celestial space
Amidst dazzling arrays of caring emotions
Perhaps we were doused with gypsy-potions?

Brighter Days

There may be brighter days ahead
How oft' have we heard that said?
I'd rather see today for what it is
Seeing this moment as mine and His.
Brighter days are 'oft overrated
Expectations leaving you frustrated,
I'll take today and love it just the same
One may never find another to claim.
More important is with whom we share
This moment… so precious and rare.

Just Because

Don't know if I'm comin' or goin'
All that chemo on the brain is tough.
Are there bills I'm still owin'?
Should I take a nap or do other stuff?

Elusive thoughts can quell unique action
Why am I sittin' here on the "throne?"
Am I here to get mental traction?
Read a book, or talk on the phone?

It makes no difference where you are
What you are doin' at the time you pause.
You've earned the right to be spatially ajar
It's okay to think: "it's simply "BECAUSE."

Clear Reflections

Some days are harder than others
Yet you stroll through with clear reflections
Spurning the dark, seeing only bright colors,
Consistent with your natural predilections.

The smile on your face, the love in your heart
Magnifies clarity and purpose of your soul
That in Your mind plays no essential part.
Emanating wholly from the ardor you extol.

You Can Fly

Believe in yourself and you can fly!
Explode above the rainy clouds
Into a world that money can't buy,
Where the air is pure, devoid of crowds.

Ascend above the inclination
That harbors destructive persuasion.
Seek true celestial stimulation
And heal despite hints of suffocation.

Unexpected Friendship

Frog went a courtin' she did go
Into the pond hither and thither
Seeking out a fine young beau,
When unseen a snake did slither.

The serpent moved to make the strike
But outta the blue the mongoose spoke:
"What I'm gonna do you won't dislike –
No idle threat, this predator's neck I broke."

A day of luck for one four-legged friend,
Not to be slashed by poisonous fangs
"For what you sow comes back in the end."
The terrified frog now 'TOAD-ALLY' sang:

RIBBIT, MY GOOD FRIEND, RIBBIT

My Baby's Back

I am grateful for my getting my "baby back"
Ribs that she lovingly pokes in a fake attack.
I'm thankful to be in love with my childhood friend
In awe that with this affliction she did not ascend.
I am grateful for the prodigious outpouring of love
Send through friends and family directly from above.
I am thankful for receiving another auspicious chance
To have my "baby back" with more advanced romance.
I am grateful the Lord granted me fortitude
To weather the storm throughout this interlude.
I am thankful for the many blessings in my life
But now most especially for my phenomenal wife.

"Sizzling" humor is a must in cancer "therapy." Here clearly my play on words is a private message designed to prepare Debbie for that night's dinner where I will prepare one of her favorite dishes. Hopefully, I won't burn it.

When First Our Eyes Met

As memory fills
From earlier days
A ride of joyful thrills
Routine on weekend days.

Sweet visions of my girl
Awaiting my arrival debut,
Let butterflies unfurl
I know what I wanna' do!

Yet through the sunlight blaze
Did I see an image there
Or just a dreamy gaze?
I could not just stop and stare.

How could I know the impact
Of such a fleeting look
Was it real, did my pulse react?
There's more to tell if I pen a book.

Friendship

What is a best friend?
Is there but one, or many?
Who do we befriend?
Were there ever any?

Too many questions—
Enigma creates panic,
Panic creates tensions
Tensions stifle romance.

No such puzzle afflicts me
Hidden romance is my miracle.
A core of emotional canopy;
No theory, my truth empirical.

My matchmaker left nothing to chance—
Our lockers side by side at thirteen
Launching the path to future romance,
Beginning solely with a friendly mien.

Our friendship blossomed as surely as a rose,
Nourished with the same tenderness and care
As laughter, trust, and honesty arose
Nurturing a warmth of which we were aware.

When all you desire is being together
Intending no secrets, seeing no faults,
Conjoined with a spiritual magic tether
Then inevitably friendship exalts

That magic we shared so long—
Transforming friendship into love
Proving friends turned lovers cannot be wrong.
Underscoring the cornerstone of true love.

While not all friendships spawn love,
Love without friendship is hollow.
The two must fit like a glove
Entwined as one forever to follow.

Ok, so maybe this is not Debbie and me. But, given Her passion for "the kiss"...if we had met at five years old, me thinks this is exactly the photo I suspect would have been taken. Ha! You laugh!

Dreams Come True

I would think as a little boy
Who will I marry later in life?
Hopefully someone I could enjoy
Perhaps she'd even love wildlife.
As a boy you dream many things,
Of money or fame, and stuff like that.
Rarely you'd focus on wedding rings,
Just where in the world you're at.
I must have been different in my own way
With thoughts of the future beyond today,
Dreaming of the girl I'd be with one day
Lacking attention to what people say.
Then it happened, I cannot say how;
Early sketches became more clear.
All of a sudden you were here and now,
We merged together on a new frontier.
Who can say where a boy's dreams will end?
The heart controls what the mind can't grasp,
Mine strayed over the rainbow and back again
Appearing at the altar in open-mouth gasp.
Sometimes the girl of your dreams appears
Out of the mist into the reality of life,
Extinguishing the worst of your fears –
Finally becoming your cherished wife.
The love we share is precious and rare
And only we know the feelings we share.
Reflecting love when into eyes we stare
Without that we'd simply be nowhere…

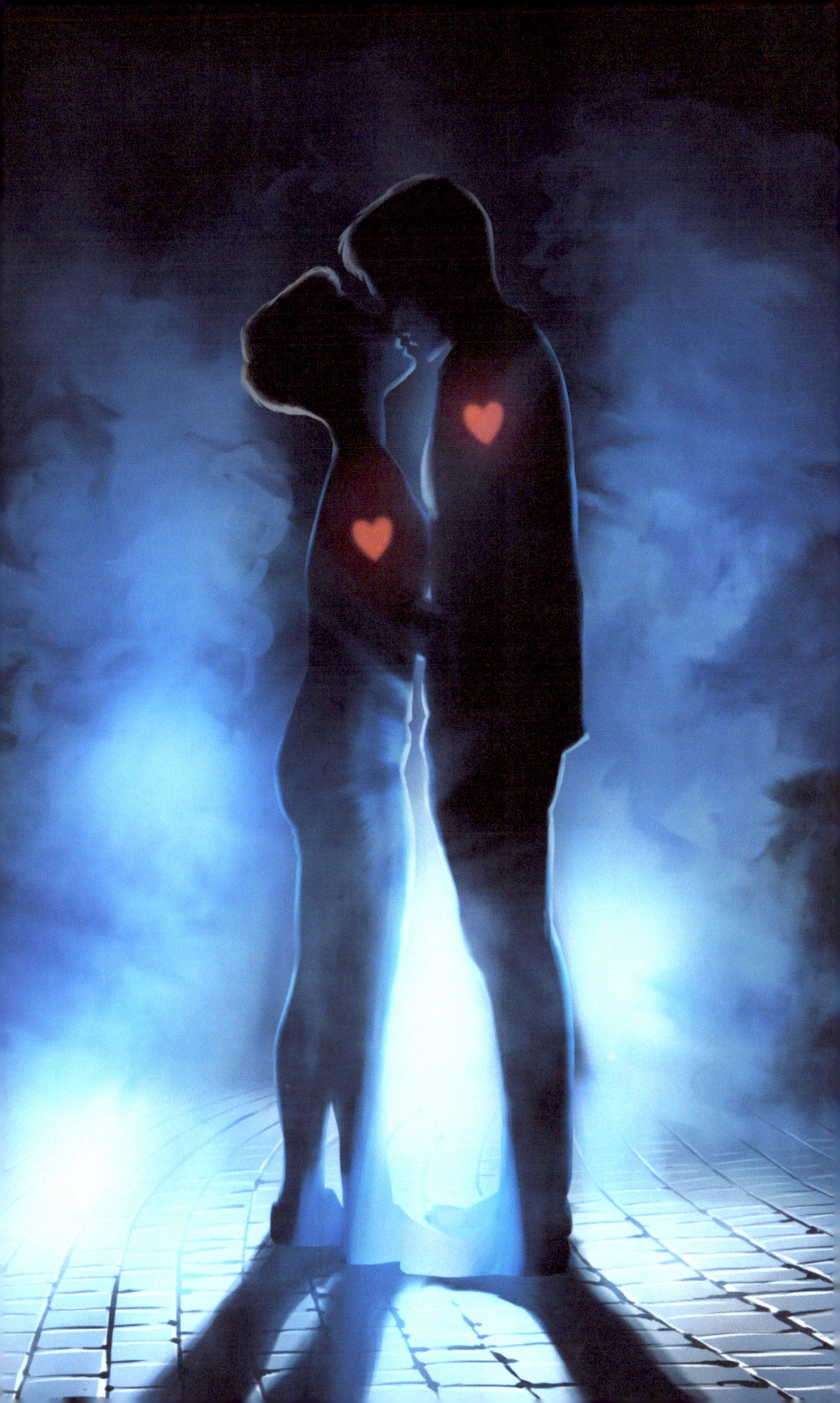

Serenity's Knife

You are amazing; that's what you are,
For no one sets a better example
Exceeding the gold standard by far –
Your impervious nature is more than ample.

Who can know what the future brings,
Thrills and bliss or chaos in life.
Yet from your soul optimism springs,
Cutting through strife with serenity's knife.

Rest Your Head

Rest your head on my shoulder
Lay your cheek against mine,
I'll be your pain holder
Between the kisses and the wine.

Unpack your baggage, fill my soul
With suff'ring that you betrays.
Let me absorb, enshroud, annul
And rescue you from malaise.

Rest your head on my chest
Lay your cheek against mine –
Allow my love to do the rest
Join my heart and the sublime.

Courage

Courage cannot be manufactured
Even with a body badly fractured,
Forming early within the womb
Cells of grit begin to bloom.

Nourished by the spirit of the divine
Weaved with threads of life spun fine,
Braided with potency, bursting into life
Charged with the mission to lessen strife.

Courage ripens, salving body and soul
Just in time our fears to control.
Never have I seen such rich display
Of courage She renders in Her rare way.

"Courage isn't having the strength to go on-it is going on when you don't have strength." Napoleon Bonaparte

---

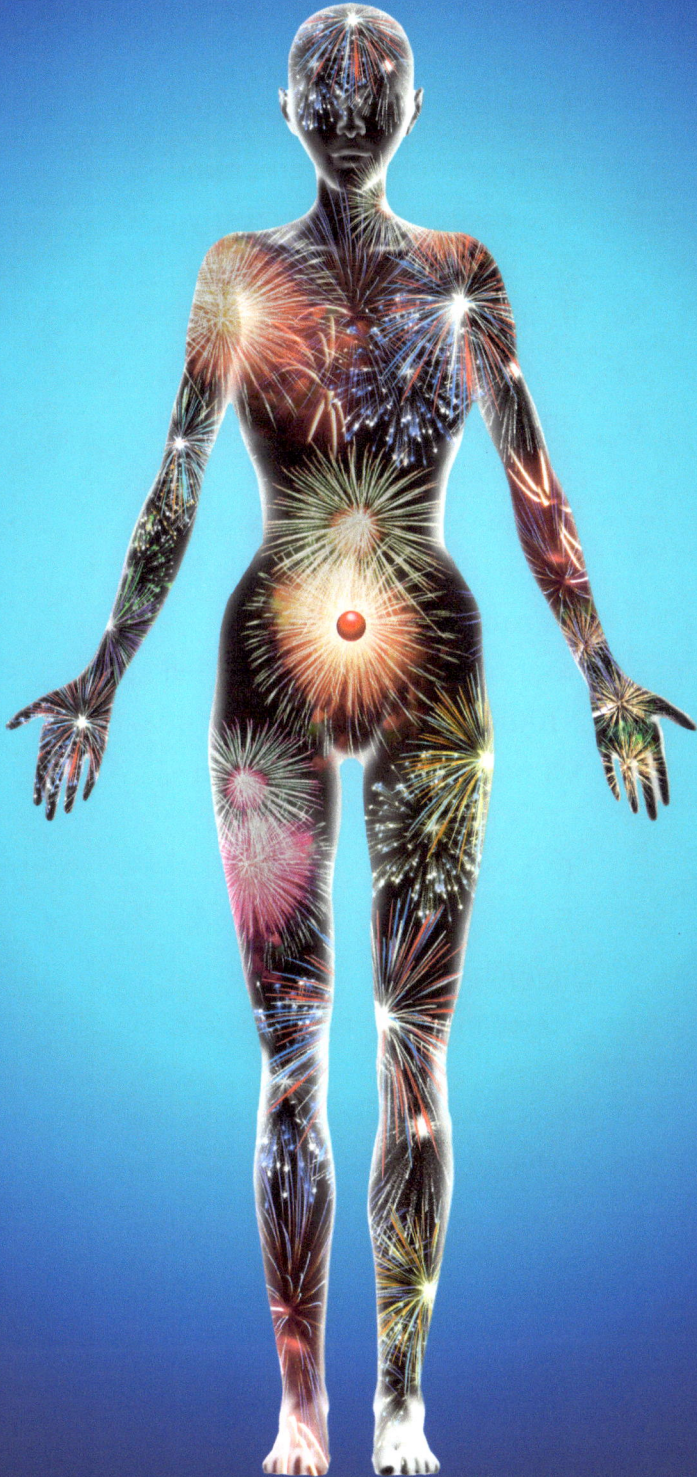

Unchained

Happy, generous and kind
A trifecta of human traits
Permeate your soul and mind
Free pass through the pearly gates?
You have the best intentions
Revealed over a lifetime
Of pernicious abstentions,
Embracing the pure and sublime –
To grow His gifts inside
Where few have the wherewithal
To use the largesse supplied
Or square accounts at all.
Your happy and humble mien
Aroused something deep inside
Of me, in truth, unforeseen
I just required satisfied...
To know I gave completely
To feel my mission attained.
Not letting fear defeat me
To see my Love unchained.

This Moment Only

As sands pour through the hourglass
I see not yesterday nor tomorrow.
On these, today I'll take a pass
It's from your playbook I'll borrow.

Keeping in touch with your eternal light
Seeping from the fabric of your soul,
Keeping you grounded with keen insight
Fixed to this moment yielding control.

Read a book, sway lazily in a hammock
Push all thoughts away for another time
Let your heart wander; let it run amuck
Reveal your true spirit, it's no pantomime.

For this day I'll mimic your movements
Nibbling delicacies of your unique designs
Borrowing shamelessly these clear improvements
Cherishing our moments, a thousand times.

"Be happy in the moment, that's enough. Each moment is all we need, not more." Mother Teresa

Let Darkness Be

Worry 'bout nil 'till the day "it" arrives,
Dream only good things coming to our lives.
For who can know what the Lord has in store
Until you strive to open that door.

Without effort you've purchased this gift,
As all around you so many fall adrift.
Yet there are some whose eyes do see
As you inspire them to let the darkness be.

"When there is darkness, dare to be the first to shine light." Steve Maraboli

My Hero

We approach the end with anticipation
Our yearning reaching highest expectation.
My heart is beating like a parade drum
Anticipating our return to a life of fun.

What a privilege watching over you,
Loving your mien as you eschew
The miasma of discomfort that cancer bestows
Still unflappable in the grip of heinous throes.

A hero is one showing great courage
Maybe suffering, but not failing to encourage.
My sweetheart is this and more to me
Serene and calm; my hero for eternity.

"As you get older it is harder to have heroes, but it is sort of necessary." Earnest Hemingway

Nothing Encumbers

Cancer cannot smother hope
Faith allows you to cope.
Cancer cannot inhibit love
Gifted by the Lord above.
Cancer cannot tarnish kindness
Cradled within your own fineness.
Cancer cannot ravage courage
Nor cause spirits to malnourish.
Cancer cannot mask sunshine's powers
Nor <u>wilt</u> the petals of exquisite flowers.
Beautiful people such as you
Often lack the strength you grew.
To power bravely all the way through.
Never stopping to "run the numbers,"
Choosing trust on which Nothing Encumbers.

Moments to Treasure

Whether we cuddle or spoon,
Both send me to the moon.
My eyes roll back and glaze
As our intimacy I praise.
It's the closeness we share
Best here than anywhere.
The most perfect antidote
To keep us both afloat.
Boosting our languor
Off-loading any anger.
Moments evoking pleasure
For us to ever treasure.

Angelic Disposition

I posted an order for a sunny day
Expecting that most certainly will occur,
You deserve a day without grey
A little gentle breeze if you prefer.

Your senses cry out for the sun
To warm your face as well as spirit.
An aspiring wish for a celestial outcome;
Should I include a song with a lyric?

I'd sing your praises of beauty and roses,
My "American Rose," its scent and splendor
Forever reminds me where our love reposes
As our auras of light together surrender.

Your mood rises in the glow of light
I've seen the evidence as the seasons change,
Both character and visage radiate bright –
An angelic glow of glorious range.

Hypnotic Aura

What is more precious than sparkling diamonds,
More beautiful than tropical islands?
None compete with your hypnotic aura
The power of your love and joy, my señora.

Forged from the core energy of life
Then shaped and woven into my dear wife.
Imbued with a simple selfless goodness,
Blended into a mix of pure happiness.

Then melted like butter onto all you greet
Ungilded, your own art form so sweet –
Sparking a giddy tingle washing over me
Enduring, singing my soul with luminosity.

How grateful am I to receive your gift
Unbidden, without which I'd be adrift.
A façade of strength in my younger days
Crumbled beneath your smiling gaze,

Replaced with love transcending my brain
So, what you see of me is but a gain.
Mixing and matching the traits that we own
Becoming each other's magic lodestone.

"It's so dark right now, I can't see any light around me. That's because the light is coming from you. You can't see it but everyone else can." Lang Leav

EEK, SQUIRREL

So, while this might be a real photo
It's NOT our mailbox, that you know.
And rather than holding a flower
This squirrel would rather it devour,
Then be on the end of my firepower

For humorous anecdote. See note #10 at Jack's Potpourri.

A Melody Without Notes

Once in a while, when I see you down
I look here and there, and all around –
Seeking visions of better days ahead,
Dispelling images of fear and dread.
I then hear the symphony of truth
Heard so often when I was a youth,
Playing a tune cutting the edges of doom
And propelling me out of my gloom.
Music for the soul without a melody
Crying out a harmonious remedy,
Screaming at me from head to my feet:
"It simply isn't in you to concede defeat."
This is your mantra, a potent refrain
Underscoring a mindset never to complain.
We see it in your face, know you are a fighter,
Inside, your core simply burns brighter.

I Am

I am the trunk to your roots
The beneficiary of your attributes.
The thunder to your lightning
Where darkness reigns before lightening.

I am the anguish to your tranquility
Sometimes displaying my imbecility.
The rock to your scintillating sapphire,
Yet undeniably a romantic outlier.

I am the beast to your beauty
Standing tall on my tour of duty;
The fever to your genuine fervor,
Tucked into your warmth I too endure.

I am the desert to your oasis
Thirsting for the safety of homeostasis.
The place where we meld our opposites,
Elevating our hearts to greater prominence.

We are the confluence of each other's evolution,
Flowing together in unending resolution.
A product of propitious history
Appearing uniquely as life's sweet mystery.

So Grateful

I'm grateful for the kindness you reveal
Entwined with hues showcasin' your appeal;
Displayed in countless ways of more sharing,
Spontaneous random acts of caring.

I'm grateful for empathy shown unbidden
Attending silent words only you hear,
Extending warmth in habits not hidden
Compassion calming my perilous fear.

I'm grateful for love dispensed equally
Unmoved by one's gender, color or speech;
Unselfish tenderness shared easily
A kiss on the cheek for each within reach.

I'm spellbound with the scale of your sweetness
Enriched with the fragrance of loveliness
Unchanging as the inviolate rose;
As He who dearly loves you, only knows.

For walking this earth with me, I'm grateful,
Transcending all layers of thankfulness –
To serve you, the ailing and the faithful
Moved deeply by your brand of happiness.

I'm grateful you chose me from the sea of men,
I'm grateful knowing love's sincerely shared.
I'm grateful at life's end we'll begin again
With our greatest gift: Friends before love declared.

"At times, our own light goes out and is rekindled by a spark from another person. Each of us has cause to think with deep gratitude of those who have lighted the flame within us." Albert Schweitzer

My Angel

Are there angels on earth to protect us?
To love, to guide, and nudge us toward a course
Of greater love and compassion to endorse;
Providing a moral compass?
Delivering heavenly messages
As God's divine helpers, radiating
Unfiltered joy into our world, elevating
Our problems to celestial triages.
Are these earth angels purely spiritual
Or incarnate walking in our midst?
If so, whose name might I put on the list?
Am I exposed to one individual
Specifically assigned as my guide?
Might I know in my soul who in my life
Holds influence where joy is rife
And searches for happiness are satisfied?
For me the choice would be uncomplicated
For seconds I'd muse, then think Debbie.
The wonderful girl I married already
For a lifetime of happiness celebrated.

Just Pretend

Pretend this is your beautiful Jake,
He'd do anything for your sake.
Like you, he knew how to roll with punches
Intuitively sensing where the crunch is.
He loved his "mommy" without any doubt,
Sometime wanting a treat, he would pout.

Yet, never was there a more loyal friend
Incarnate now, he'd be here to defend.
Fight and claw he'd deftly engage those paws
And if necessary, lock down his jaws.
Whatever you needed, he'd be there for you
Together, we'd adhere to you like glue.

The Real Beloved Jake
1986 – 2000

"Until one has loved an animal, a part of one's soul remains unawakened."
Anatole France

Share Your Glow

The sweetness in your face
A kindness in your soul –
A spirit full of grace,
Who fails to see your whole?

You cannot see what I see:
Exemplar of a perfect woman.
Your fullness flowing over me
In casks of emollient to summon,

To soothe my aching heart
As salve encasing fear and anguish –
Engaged to break my soul apart,
Then must I pledge not to languish.

Embrace your glow, a mix of angel's purity
Eschew clouds of darkness, torrents and gale
Enriched to thrash my insecurity,
Invite troves of love whence your virtues hail.

Chase the Rainbows

In times of towering adversity
Why don't we see demonstrability?
Of advantages in opportunity
And virtues of greater propinquity.

Plain as the puddles of pouring rain
We surely will not render insane,
With only something priceless to gain
Beholding friendships hard to maintain.

Stay close, remain in each other's shadows
Become prolonged friends, seek not in
between.
Hand in hand pursue and chase the rainbows
Create intimacy; make friends feel seen.

Accept exposure to getting hurt.
Rewards of closeness offers remedies,
If love results it will not you desert
Fulfilling dreams and whispers of fantasies.

Soulmates

Who can describe what we call a soulmate,
Someone with whom you join by fate?
Does she cut her eyes at you incognito?
But you noticed her face is all aglow.
Do you start a sentence and she ends it,
Or simply smiles, afraid to commit?
Are you tethered as one in spirit,
Or distinct but equal as you merit?
Can you live alone without the other,
Or spend your life chasing one another?
Knowing these answers doesn't make you smart
But does confirm what's in your heart.
And stirs your soul that's all aquiver:
A symphony of love that makes you shiver.

"Do you believe, as I do, that our souls spoke, long before our lips ever got a chance to?" Sayed H. Fatimi

Let It Go

On occasion could we just reverse time?
So, She can simply avoid the long climb,
Replay the life so complex and sublime.

Revert to sippy cups and safe slumber
Forego big girl pants, She shan't go under,
Eschew all thoughts that seek to encumber.

Let's make it easy, not fall in the trap
We don't need sippy cups to take that nap,
Just snuggle up, and I'll lay on Her lap.

When naps increase delightfully with age,
Does our fighting ethos drop from the stage?
Resilience falter seeking to disengage?

Nay, big girl pants will be there tomorrow,
For now, catharsis you must seek or borrow
The promise of calm shall not we embargo.

So put them on or take them wisely off –
Inaction only leads to null tradeoff,
And neither provides sufficient payoff.

Decide not, secure that fluffy pink throw –
Forget all options, to dreams say hello.
Sleep my darling, and just let it all go.

Spiritual Brakes

Our life comes at us, never slowing down
Applying brakes is a great endeavor.
Must we push the pedal to avoid breakdown?
Yet to spiritual brakes, say no, never.

Your mien of peace leavens the soul's relief
Catching your breath indulging life's nectar.
Eschewing the wild tempest of grief
Priceless: the worth of a cancer defector.

Shift the gears of spiritual surrender
Release the brakes on the Lord's grace,
Tap the fuel to emotional splendor
Unlock His power with your smiling face.

Your Bright Light

While God is wise, faithful and love,
You are strong, positive, and deserving –
Of His gifts so characteristic of
One given her life to serving,
All the wants and needs of others:
Friends, husband, kids, and mothers
Before meeting any of your own druthers.
Your love shines bright over all that it covers.

Stronger Together

I really love who you are
And who I am when I'm with you.
Our friendship has grown stronger by far
As have our vows since we uttered "I do."

Some folks might utter the words
While thinking of the honeymoon
And not on the meaning of the verbs,
Reflecting later if they spoke too soon.

The ties of our alliance
Held firm as the months turned to years,
While upgrading our self-reliance
As "I do" in fond memory appears.

These words were our synergy
Organic lyrics that sparked our birth
To fuel our souls with the energy
Transcending limits of heaven and earth.

We are a phalanx of two.
We stand as an army of one –
Impervious in our strength anew
Together fighting a battle, we won.

Shrouded in Goodness

Your recipe for sweetness will not be found
'Cause kindness weaves within your cellular core.
Indelible humble traits simply astound
And underscores all of you that we adore.

The threads your essential character evokes
Reveals the pure soul with which you are blessed,
The golden warps and silver fills reveal coats
That cloaks appearance of breasts that are stressed

Yet worry not on minor surface visuals.
You are so much more than the sum of your parts –
It's what makes us special as individuals
And loved especially for what's in our hearts.

Throughout ordeals where lessers wither and fade
Your mantle glows as a virtuous beacon,
A clear exemplar of kindness unbetrayed:
And a passion marshalled never to weaken.

Neither days nor nights pass where kindness abates –
Ne'er hood nor shroud blocks the light shining through,
As you have a face that time cannot erase
Who knows better than She, when you say, "I love You?"

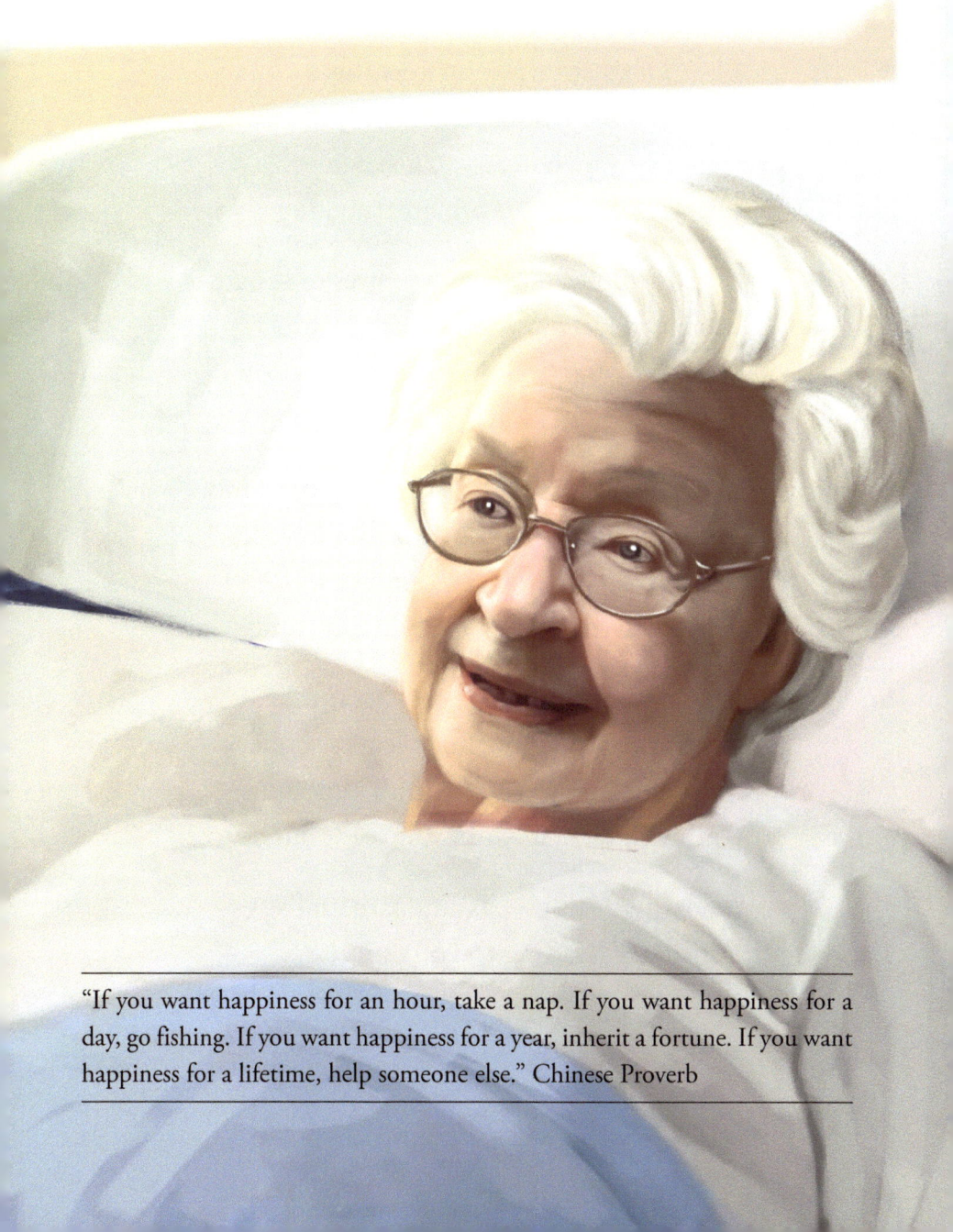

"If you want happiness for an hour, take a nap. If you want happiness for a day, go fishing. If you want happiness for a year, inherit a fortune. If you want happiness for a lifetime, help someone else." Chinese Proverb

A Laughing Matter

Why keep frogs outta your pants?
'Cause they're worse than small pesky ants,
Not as bad as dreaded poison ivy
That really makes you itch and whiny.

Best not to store any critters there
Causes more trouble than you can bear.
Other smart choices you are taking
Displays of courage are breathtaking.

This mental picture of creatures on-board
Must not in your mem'ry be stored,
A mere distraction preempting reaction
Toward otherwise the main attraction.

Have not I now made you laugh out loud?
Forsaking all thoughts now disallowed,
My outrageous and salty humor
May even dissipate a mean brain tumor.

One might assign that only to rumor
That's okay if your cancer leaves sooner.
They say laughter is good for the soul
And wonderfully, briefly, favors your parole.

Releasing fear, by-passing pain and stress
Ultimately leading to your success...
So let your guard down with a hearty laugh,
And I'll share the burden on your behalf.

"Power, money, persuasion, supplication, persecution-these can lift at a colossal humbug – push it a little – weaken it a little, century by century, but only laughter can blow it to rags and atoms at a blast. Against the assault of laughter nothing can stand." Mark Twain

My Nectar for Life

As the hummingbird wings so often flutter
So does my heart beat to show I love her.

The sweetness of nectar so vital for life
Flows naturally from a bouquet's that's rife.

With redolence of delicate flowers in bloom
And essence of a soul evoking perfume,

This world of mine's made better by you
Aflutter with knowing how our love is true.

As the birds spread the ambrosia for birth
So does my Sweetheart sow love to the earth...

My Love

You are love, my love
Yet You share that love.
All you know benefit
With a smile starlit,
Dispensed equally
With grace and beauty.

With kindness replete
Making It so sweet –
Laced with humble pie
I breath a full sigh,
Breathless for all time.
Life's no pantomime.

A best friend for life
Radiant jewel, my wife,
Accepts who I am
Faults and sins, yes ma'am.
I am so enriched...
Agog... we got hitched.

"Anyone can be passionate, but it takes real lovers to be silly." Rose Franken

Wellspring

Once in a while in the early morn'
Senses linger in rosy sunshine,
Bluegreen water does my mind adorn
Drifting down an elegant coastline.

In the ebb and flow of daily life
It's easy of life's favor to miss,
Entangled in the turmoil of strife
How oft have we forfeited the kiss?

The one I love knows not of such loss
Inhaling nature's beauty and spring flowers.
Available and willing to bear others' cross
In spite of hardships, nuances or hours.

Embracing life with a tender kiss
Not apt to miss the best of life's flow,
Meandering through grassy knolls of bliss –
In harmony with where God's footsteps go.

This love of life brought forward from birth,
Combines joy and boundless passion:
Her Wellspring of sublime moral worth,
Dispensed in her singular fashion.

Wellspring: an abundant source of continual supply or emanation (Merriam-Webster Dictionary)

His Aura

He's 'specially close to you right now
How do I know? I just do somehow.
The energy, your radiant smile
That always does me sweetly beguile.
He knows your mien of utter kindness:
Ignoring faults of less esteemed, egoless
Dispensing abundant caring love.
As He watches blithely from above –
He sees the selfless acts emitting
And recognizes you never quitting.
Fulfilling purpose meant only for you
His shining temple to emulate too.
No other explanation makes sense –
His aura surrounding you is immense.

Jumpstart My Heart

You are my angel; you are my sweetheart:
Iconic spirit and flesh mixed and blended
Who never fails to jumpstart my heart
Dispensing love in ways all too splendid.

I never could endure life without you,
An angel with wings only I can see
Imbued by God with goodness all the way through
Navigating the sea of life peacefully.

Traversing turbulent winds and sharks below
Adroitly sidestepping tempests of our times,
To trim the sails, "heave to," as frighten' sailors know
My eyes see, my soul feels, how your spirit climbs.

I wish profoundly I were more like you,
Contented and sated with the joy life brings
Living now, seeing how, emerging anew.
Whence such tranquil moments your grandeur springs.

Always Happy

She lays there bundled in her fluffy throw
So lovable, huggable, kissable
Saying chemo wasn't so bad as foes go –
So honest, so irresistible.
So many days, too many months racing
In seemingly tight circles of frantic
Mind bracing, feet pacing, and life facing
Contests bereft of something romantic.
In God's best of worlds where love reigns supreme
The vista she sees transparently clear
Seeps with joy and, oh yes, vanilla ice cream.
Covertly I must dab a secret tear.
She questions not "Why," nor cancer's ubiquity.
Instead, shedding fear as snakes molt outer skin
Innately knowing risks of antipathy,
Adopting only healthy thoughts from within.
This rare asylum springs from her core
Encircling every thought; every action
Elevated, shielding her that much more
From mental trauma and joyful contraction.
Her happiness is not fake nor phony
But a joyful appearance of inner soul,
Endowed by God as her testimony
That happy people are in full control.

"Happiness cannot be traveled to, owned, earned, worn or consumed. Happiness is the spiritual experience of living every minute with love, grace, and gratitude." Denis Waitly

Cheating Death

I believe She's crafted ways to cheat death
Betting life savings Death is most wary
Exhaling sighs of melancholy breath,
Afraid of strong Will that's legendary
For her customary thrust and parry.
Precisely catching opponents off guard
With blows of mirth delivered contrary
Escaping vestiges of darkness barred.
Alone Her mien appears inadequate
Combined however with a steely will
She'll fight to the death, no matter what –
"Ignore This cancer devil at your peril."
A surer defense than bullets and swords
The shield emerges largely from Her soul,
Distinct from physical prowess or wards
The place where she never loses control.

Nothing's gonna drag me down to a death that's not worth cheating. – *Author: Elliott Smith*

In Spain, however, people have found a way of **cheating death**. They summon it to appear in the afternoon in the bull ring, and they make it face a man. Death – a fighting bull with horns as weapons - is killed by a bullfighter. And the people are there watching death being cheated of its right. – *Author: Maia Wojciechowska*

One Rose Too Many?

A single rose for one life saved by God.
Two stems identify love and courage,
Trifecta adds one more fragrance to applaud;
Quartets bespeak joy we must encourage.
The quintet is nearly enough for a vase –
Half dozen is quarter way to getting lucky.
Full dozen e'er sees a smile on her face,
The magic of twenty-four; oh, so gutsy.
Anniversaries call for larger urns
Showcasing one for every year of love.
You're looking for a blush on her that burns
En route to the bedroom we can't speak of.
Bestowing copious cascading Roses
Each year exceeding nosegays before,
Expecting response more than she discloses –
Silly me for thinking she must keep score.
At thirty years with similar outcome
Even a novice begins to detect
Clear signs inciting his brain to go numb,
And many years of suspect to dissect.
With so much of my life still yet to live
I listened carefully to what she said.
"I know you grant what's in the heart to give,
Yet ponder the nature of love instead."
Forgoing gifts of unchanging value

Does one more rose add a kiss to the vase,
Rekindle sparks always meant to be true?
Can you foresee just a poem in their place?
A slow learner for sure; but learn I can.
Instead of bouquets a single rose comes
Attended happily with poems by her man;
Accompanied too with a kiss without sums.

Pretty much a true story, with a bit of paraphrasing of Debbie. At least the way
I perceived her comments and reaction. Additionally, I cut this Mr. Lincoln very
fragrant rose from one of our bushes and snapped a selfie which I presented to
my wonderfully talented artist, Elena, from Belarus. She painted a marvelous
"me" despite having little to work with. The rose speaks for itself.

Fruits of Labor

Peach, rhubarb and strawberry jam
I love them way better than any old yam.
Lather the bread with all you can
Leave it to Sweetie, and then scram.
All that you cook we'll not exam
Unless perhaps you forgot to use pam.
And sugar is a must, as you know ma'am,
Picking one "fruity" on a desert island to cram
It must be your apple pie, hot damn!

For humorous related anecdote see note # 8, Jack's Potpourri

Most Potent Recipe

Beauty is not just texture of skin,
Gracious facades or pageants you win.
But transcends barriers of your physique;
Revealing what makes you truly unique.
Casting indelible glow from deep inside

Showcasing a side you cannot hide.
Intrinsic beauty includes so much:
Kindness, compassion, love and such,
Collectively exalting the core of our soul.
Yet, must have strength to fully bankroll.
For beauty and strength jointly belong
In the recipe we must ever prolong.

One without the other, while divine,
Cannot compete with assets we combine.
Beauty and strength my sweetheart dispenses
A scrumptious soufflé blending all of her senses.
As best dishes comprise fresh ingredients
Personal virtues embody crucial nutrients

That armor the soul in times of distress,
Isolate anger disease may possess
And keep alive confidence and patience –
While tending to sickness in all patients.
In this world of chaos and cancer anecdotes
Your strength and beauty are perfect antidotes.

"An eagle earns its honor from the storms it endures." Matshona Dhliwayo

Hum of Joy

I think I heard you hum just now
So low I might even have missed
A tune played when first we kissed
As surely both we're sensing wow.
It truly is remarkable
In view of days we spend in hell,
As science cast its healing spell
Until meters show you're full.
That the little girl inside unfolds
With youthful winsome innocence
Unscrambled by acquiescence –
Unveiling the calm she holds.
A hum bespeaks of inner peace
Tranquility personified;
In rarified tones amplified
And bids the sickness cease.
The joy I feel in so hearing
The sounds of struggle harmonized,
Expanding my soul uncompromised
Keepin' my fear disappearin'.
I've always known this little girl
Absorbed the strength of her angel's core
While sins of sadness she'd ignore;
Perhaps I'll give humming a whirl.

"It takes a very long time to become young." Pablo Picasso

"He will command his angels concerning you, to guard you," Luke 4:10

Seventy-Two Hours

Seventy-Two hours until blastoff
The fuel is nearly expended
Distinctive new lopes display the payoff,
This demon's totally upended.
We're so excited; in cardiac spasm
Your team is ready, the scans are clean.
Emerge my dear from this painful chasm
In newfangled attire you'll be seen.
Agony gone; dignity restored
Gone is the awkward ungainly gait,
Remodeled by the grace of the Lord
With family and friends on you to wait.
Seventy-two hours to see the rear view
Through prisms that display the joys of living
Engage to dream on what you'll pursue:
Giving thanks and loving family at Thanksgiving?

IN ALL THINGS
give
thanks

FINITO

Today is your last chemo infusion,
Faring well is a foregone conclusion.
You are anxious for this to be over,
And soon will be laying in tall, sweet clover.
Has been a rugged journey at the least,
Regrettably needed to tame this beast.
Your Friends and family are oh so proud
You never bowed your head nor woefully cowed,
As all of our love does your soul enshroud.

Yes, Debbie actually did wear her hair long, from age 19 to 32. Our children
were 3 (Jaime) and 6 (Michael) and when she cut it, they were most unhappy,
saying "You don't look like mommy anymore." In my mind beautiful either style.

Our Steadfast Journey

Our journey is over, the pain behind us
The travel to and 'fro no longer a fuss,
The year of eternity we all feared –
Hit like a tsunami and then disappeared.
A man cannot fathom a woman's breasts bereft
With unequaled surgeon's skill, we see no theft.
How you coped with that and much more.
It pierced my soul as inward I swore.
Ne'er for physical loss did I lament
Merely sad at what we hoped to prevent,
Yet cancer speaks in a foreign tongue
The translation: bad news on us had sprung.
Chemo and rads in your body were strewn
"Allowing" sleep well into the afternoon,
When the fog of treatment dulled you emerged
Casting brilliant hues as energy surged.
Our souls became one to fight this intrusion
Defeating the threat was a foregone conclusion,
When two hearts merged and beat as one
There was cancer... and then there was none.
You faced the devil and stared it down
It battled hard, now its ship's aground,
There's no fire that withstands the torrent:
Together we signed its death warrant.
For the heat of love trumps the embers of evil

We are winners over the devil Primeval!
And so, my darling together we rise,
Approaching the zenith of love, our prize.
I lack the words, sufficient or wise
To convey the pride that my heart cries,
For the strength of your soul the Lord endowed
I'm eternally His servant, head gratefully bowed.

"Love is composed of a single soul inhabiting two bodies." Aristotle

PART II

These poems, written in private moments and not shared with Debbie during her treatments, contain deep feelings of fear, pain, melancholy and finally, victory, with some other emotions thrown in. My glass half-empty side slowly splashed its contents up and over the top. I was able to work my way through some emotional wreckage, and anger that emerged after believing this demon had been defeated. And in the ensuing weeks the weight on my heart lifted and the poems began to take on a different tone. One embracing more positive territories of love, acceptance and even gratitude. Not, of course, for the weight of cancer lifting, since that wasn't certain, but for the blessings of past times and hope for similar ones in the future. While my "job" centered on uplifting Debbie, in fact the opposite rang true as well, most especially each day as I absorbed her joy and positivity reading my poems aloud. This dark side of me is not easy to reveal. And had it not lifted, perhaps I would not be so quick to share. With such diverse simultaneous emotions washing and sloshing against each other one had to surface and clean the others. I am grateful for my inner angel winning the battle.

Screams of Anguish

The maelstrom of your cancer plagues my soul
Who pulls the strings, who's in control?
What solution exists but quiet submission?
Oh Lord, is there no cause for remission?

Silent screams echo from the walls of my heart
Stifled ululating lurks to break me apart,
Plunging over the great falls without protection
Over mind or emotion; endless, rejection.

Can I withstand more trepidation?
Or transcend feelings of lamentation?
Am I not best in focus on solutions,
Distilling problem sets into resolutions?

'Me' cannot exist in this sullied life's chapter
To an inward focus I will not be captor.
Mental ablutions must cleanse self-pity
Add many tasks to keep myself busy.

Erect that barrier with which I'm acquainted
Erase the memories from which I'm tainted.
Transform the sunlight as do the flowers
To ribbons of colors displaying Your powers.

Absorb the might lost by my Love
And reflect it back as if from God above,
To project this small beacon of strength
And find a peace that will come at length.

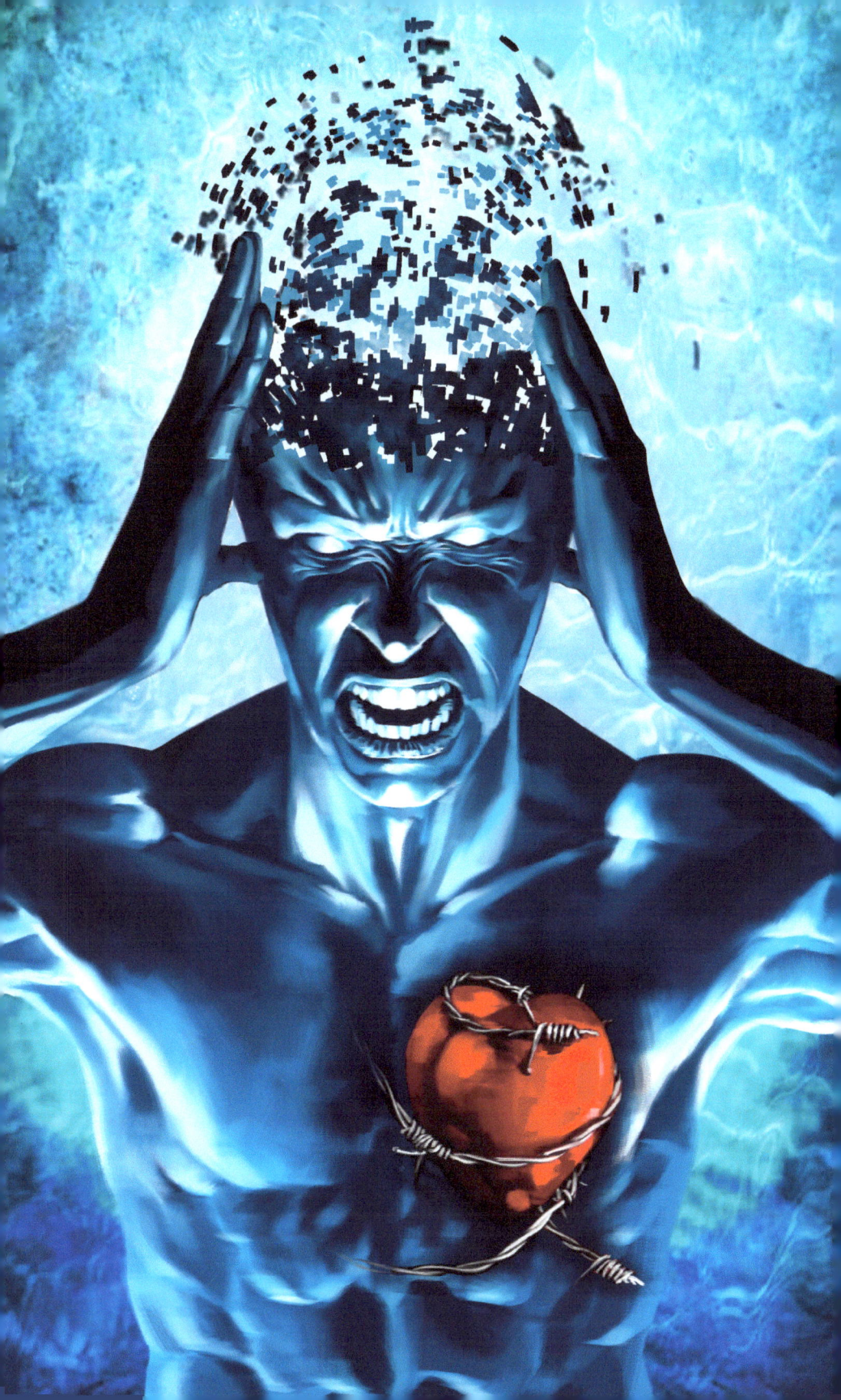

Hidden Fears

Hidden fears are well obscured
Years of emotional walls inured,
Unceasing anguish endured
Now the walls are unsecured.

The truth is a snake of many strains
With sharp fangs; fear coursing in my veins
Angst pumped to blood and brains
How much more of true-me remains?

"When you are inspired by some great purpose, some extraordinary project, all your thoughts break their bonds." Pantanjali, circa 100 BC

Can I escape this swamp of hell
Pushing me ever towards the death knell –
Is there anyone whom I should tell?
Nay, strengthen the walls inside where I dwell.

Well-hidden 'til I am freed from thrall
To answer Your service each time You call,
Anguish rendered, the darkness I'll stall
Bringing me far away from fear and all.

Impervious walls long sustained are forfeit
Completely rend I'm happy to admit.
If I'm not all in, unwilling to commit
Then surely, I'm naught but a hypocrite.

Provoked into action when my head rings
With gentle reminders to unfold your wings,
Help you soar without thought nor care
To see the smile knowing I'll always be there.

Suffocation

Excise demons aimed to plunder my soul,
Defy the searing melancholy toll
Engulfing, suffocating my peace of mind
Destroying heart and soul with core entwined.

Tendrils of panic wrap around my chest
Happiness fights for space amidst the dread,
Sighing for times when I can simply rest
Gasping to regain composure that fled.

Assailed from all directions taking blows,
Then deep inside from whence it comes...suppose
I seize the smallest measure of solace
Rejecting mental monsters, and say yes!

Say yes to sate chasms of desperation
Say no to emotional deprivation
Eschew forlorn self-pitying twaddle,
Restore the mentally strong role model.

I lost my way becoming paralyzed
As my conscious brain became traumatized,
Thus, fear and ire and pain now must be slain.
Regaining my honor, in faith I remain.

"When it's hard to run to light, jog; when it's hard to jog, walk; when it's hard
to walk, limp; when it's hard to limp, crawl. As long as you are headed to light,
the shackles of darkness are left behind." Matshona Dhilwayo

Knives of Grief

Knives of grief fly into my body
Releasing pain and fear they embody –
And panic drips freely like rain from a rose
Invading my core like no one knows.
At last, have I crossed my Rubicon?
Please Lord let not fear become my Krypton,
While toxins of angst cascade over me
Resisting becomes my priority.
Encircled with vultures awaiting their prey
I simply can't wish they will go away,
Regardless of my penchant to pray
A plan's essential for them to slay.
Incoming daggers are tough to parry
No time to get leery and tarry.
My life depends on a clever artifice
A foolproof strategy making them miss.
Deep down into my soul pursuing
Escape and freedom from my undoing –
I see the path; I feel a remedy.
For I am merely my own worst enemy.
To wit, I must draw courage facing my fear:
The woman I love has cancer reappear –
My fear being alone; my scare suspecting
I can't protect the soul God's perfecting.
There's only one way to break the trend:
Put all my faith in my very best friend.
Keep fear sequestered, locked and tethered,
Tomorrow we'll have this storm weathered.

"The Lord is close to the brokenhearted and saves those who are crushed in spirit." Psalm 34:18 (NIV)"

Soul-Mind-Heart

My Soul cannot quell the voices
Nor silence cacophonous noises,
Show the depth of my tremble
Nor penchant to disassemble.

My Mind alerts to disturbance
And pain with more resurgence,
The cause not always forthcoming
Confusion heightens mind numbing.

My Heart argues with the body,
Dire dialogue helps nobody
When shadows of malcontent seep
Over me even as I sleep.

This trifecta defines our essence
Helps avoid spiritual evanescence,
If my angst perceives no limits
I can't be fixed with mere gimmicks.

Engagement of heart, mind and soul.
Unique bastions I must control
If ever I hope fear to assuage,
And silence my capricious rage.

No Time for Tears

There can be no tears on the outside –
My secret grief has no safe outlet
Cannot allow my morale to slide
More time for that later, just not yet.
My heart is a chasm of fear and pain,
My soul's kindling to the fires of grief
Do I cling to the edge of insane?
Can anguish taper to sweet relief?
Or yield to this emotional maelstrom
Of malevolent wicked misery
That I must eventually shrink from
To escape the victim; to snatch victory.
To see Her in chaotic turmoil
Inflames my senses, engenders burning
That must be extinguished dampening the roil.
Obliged to find the tools, see tides turning.
Emotional arsenals of weapons
Will silence chaos, restore order
Regain usefulness as she beckons.
Destroy the pernicious boarder.
Only I can expunge the seedy devil –
Only I am armed for mortal combat
To slay those in the battle who revel.
My King against the pawns, let's start with that.

Effusion of Inner Beauty

Your inner beauty stirs my deep ardor,
Thanks offered in my daily devotions –
Kind, humble, generous, traits to armor
And blunt the edge of my darkest emotions.
There is no honor self-locked in darkness
Especially awash with lights from you.
There must be remedies quelling madness
To jettison shadows, and escape to debut
A new me, imbued with fresh energies
To share the armor you wear preserving
My precious fragile sensibilities,
Even with a life so undeserving.
Your gift of inner beauty dampens fear
Outflanks decent into mental chaos,
Expunges pity long to disappear
As apparitions of a ghostly séance.
Intrinsic chain mail thrusts to the surface
Extending thick veneers of layered steel;
Immutable force speaking with purpose
Cascading outward as afar I feel.
I summon you my dear to consecrate
Our union, pouring your marrow of light
Into this soul of melancholy substrate –
Forever sparking my core to glow bright.
Nay, summon not darling, it's my cross.
I ask too much for gifts enough given
I shan't confer to you this albatross,

Your faith alone will see this foe riven.
Like two planets orbiting each other
Our gravities' pulling us together.
Each woven in spirit to one another
Surviving ever this stormy weather.

"In the depth of winter, I finally learned that within me, there lay an invincible summer." Albert Camus

Elusive Visions

In predawn under sheets in light slumber
When fog of sleep doth thoughts encumber;
The pain is not yet rend asunder
Yet threatens still to pull me under.
I can't save her, how 'bout me, I wonder?
Yet, I simply cannot surrender –
To negative thoughts that outnumber
The means to silence the scornful thunder.

A Predator Rebuked

We're facing a ravenous predator
Insatiable hunger that we can sense.
For anyone a great competitor,
A gnawing of malice that's so intense
Creating fear that knits into our bones.
Unutterable darkness creeping nigh
Trying to destroy what It thinks It owns
While we pray and await our Lord's reply.
Together we fight this pretentious bitch
Intent to flee the wretched tsunami
Of grief and sorrow escorting this witch;
Returning It to burn eternally.
While hopes and dreams appear in jeopardy
Our means to freedom rests upon our faith;
Tenacious trust is our indemnity.
Imagine our joy as we cheat death's wraith.
Without collapse of our heart and spirit;
Eschewing fear, embracing the parts of us
Conflated with courage we did inherit.
We'll send that demon to hell, victorious.

Hailstorm

My Sweetheart has weathered the storm,
Absorbed poison and radiation hailstorm
With her unique radiant art-form:
Inherent strength that has kept her warm.

I too am rescued from the darkness,
What do I owe for this deep catharsis?
Saving me from emotional carcass,
And from sinking deep into madness.

I cracked a little but never broke
Inhaling healing celestial smoke
That swept my soul; my angels awoke
Imbuing solace, His great masterstroke.

Your Protector

I'll be your protector on the front line
Against the odds I will stand in Its way
To pass your suff'ring to the most Divine.
Relax your body tenderly against mine
Without fear nor anger, cast them away
I'll be your protector on the front line.
Our life together has been by design
A Soldier's task to guard his flock and pray
To pass your suff'ring to the most Divine.
My heart of steel joins with love to consign
Your fiercest advocate into the fray
I'll be your protector on the front line.
When all seems lost our souls will align
As I engulf your pain without delay
To pass your suff'ring to the most Divine.
There's naught of magic I won't design
No sickness too grave that I'd decline
I'm always your protector on the front line
To pass your suff'ring to the most Divine

A Game You Cannot Lose

I watch her try so hard to stay awake
To finish one more game of Word with Friends
In a game bereft of any real stake
Unsure she finishes as sleep descends?

Her head begins to drop ever so slight
A tilt, a jerk, can she be drifting off?
Will she succumb to the dark of the night?
Should I disturb her with a scratchy cough?

I feel her need to test the intellect
A trial to stimulate her mind and essence,
And mighty struggle to keep her head erect;
An Ideal metaphor for her quintessence.

Stung hard by ravages chemo made standard
Faith is the currency that has saved her.
With grit dispensed on the path meandered
A blend of gifts He gathered to confer.

The true test lies not in wakeful tenure,
Nor negotiations seeking bountiful outcomes
Or pleading bargains for Him to surrender;
But Trusting when that ocean of doubt comes.

Awakened

One goal in my life remains elusive.
Will I attain it? also inconclusive.
So many checked off, as yet.
Educated-check; career-check; family-check.

Only struggle gives us perspective,
Without this we're still defective.
Frenetic pace of our lives can foil
Intentions, aiding others to uncoil.

Without diversions common to youth,
There's more time to seek out the truth:
To learn, to discern life's purpose—
Digging deep below rough surface.

When the ice of life is chipped away,
Revealing doubt we must counterweigh,
All that's left is for us to awaken
Seeing the path not formerly taken.

Dispensing bounties left incomplete—
Showering all the people we meet,
Giving of ourselves too often bereft
Are we worried there'll be nothing left?

So, fear not what They might think
As we from the cup of gallantry drink.
Awakened to the wants of kindness,
No longer can we feign blindness.

If laying it on the line is too sublime;
Leaving all on the field stands tests of time
Saving shards of love to last spend
Is an utterly barren dead end.

As I march into the fray of lives ignored
I see the ghosts of those most adored.
And forfeit myself to those deserving
In harmony with the souls I am serving.

With these arrows in my quiver
And to my "loves" I'm a caregiver,
My careful plan's not to miss my target:
But hold my breath and simply enlarge it.

At the end of the day on my deathbed whence I lay,
I must believe that I did not betray
Buried instincts with preventable delay.
But Awaken to "my aim" before judgement day.

A Life Fulfilled

Of all my friends my wife is clearly best
From thirteen, melding closely merging souls –
What gift enriches more? I'm plainly blessed.
Expanding love as hot as burning coals
At length becoming envied man and wife.
Bestowed with children heavenly dispatched
Intent to serve a military life
Of service to country, thankful and proud.

Yet happy times can sometimes go askew
Disrupting warm halcyon memories
Without apparent cause, appeal or ado.
As life's too brief to dwell on miseries,
My Sweetheart's measure of a wicked disease
Includes oceans of faith the devil can't seize.

Debbie beautiful at Thirteen

Lieutenant Colonel Jack Stevenson, Battalion Commander of the first contingent of U.S. Army Soldiers to deploy to this theater of operations Operation Desert Storm, somewhere in Kuwait, Saudi Arabia or Iraq August 1990-April 1991

Sweetie and My Sweetheart

She carries burdens hidden well in smiles
Without unwrapping tears nor spelling doom,
Bathed in hope, the days in peace she beguiles
And calms when sweetness would her voice assume.

Pursuing not pathos nor sympathy
She senses sadness palpably beyond,
With "Sweetie" haunted with great empathy
Adding love and vigor to their sacred bond.

I watch with simple joy their chit chat speak
Refilling souls with sanguine seas of hope,
A daily diet filled with games they seek
And surging laughter ever strong to cope.

One hundred ways her Mom, her amulet,
Amazingly inspires unswerving faith
Love and hope to engender and beget.
A buoyed soul, the ultimate failsafe.

My Love decrypts the subtle evidence
Of pent-up fear in faceted sad eyes,
Dispensing daughter's love sans providence
Enjoying Sweetie's love and daily surprise.

With thanks for giving one more day of life
To sharpen edges of memories lost
Where joyful vistas of family were rife,
Amidst confluence of life's rivers both crossed.

"Youth fades; love droops; the leaves of friendship fall; A mother's secret hope outlives them all." Oliver Wendell Holmes

The Little Girl Inside

The pretty young woman I married
Unshaken with hardships she's carried,
Never lost that lovely little girl
Inhabiting like a seaside pearl.
Her temperament's calm and relaxed
Misread too oft as weakness perhaps.
That girl I know, has perfect esprit
Appearing daily for me to see.
Infectious laughter, a twinkling eye
The smallest vapor, a kiss goodbye –
Tickles the bone we might call funny
Cheap fun for no amount of money.
Ready to burst into the open
Bright shiny, a spirit unbroken,
Expressing every single new thought
With laughter and passion likewise wrought.
Who knows what makes little girls unique,
Are they similar in Mozambique?
With hyperactive wondering eyes
Effervescence comes as no surprise.
We love their quizzical simple charm,
The sauciest way to say and rearm
Why mommy, why daddy-why-why-why?
Repetition makes you wanna' cry.

Debbie at Five Years Old,
doves & batting

All of the activities associated with this poem are one's that Debbie "the tomboy" enjoyed. Yes, she climbed trees; yes, she played baseball with the neighborhood boys. And while only some of these no longer enjoy the same status, the joy they conveyed as a little girl has not disappeared. While some activities have been replaced with others, the same twinkle in her eyes, a playful giggle, a warm radiant glow, insatiable curiosity and kindness bestowed; all remain. A rare combination of little girl and woman that our Lord gifted to me and humanity as a treasure trove of joyful love.

It's in their nature to cuddle and hug
Adults might view this habit a drug
There's bunnies and puppies and birds, oh my
Forever kept without saying goodbye
Vivacious the smile while picking fruit
To fields then trees, her friends she'd recruit
So many ripe, so little time, exhausted
Leaving daylight for more fun unaccosted.
You watch them engage the fun in life
 With gusto launching new skills sans strife,
Astride a bike, ahead of the boys –
Astride life are a little girl's joys.
They dance their way into your heart
Uniquely kept from all others apart,
A union formed without accident
Conferred per God's divine sacrament.
Cuddly little girls always grow up
At length giving up their sippy cup,
Yet scents of their fragrance will linger
Past putting a ring on their finger.
 My grown-up girl retains vim and verve
Along with rarer traits she did preserve –
The perfect blend of woman and girl
Whose loving kiss is purer than pearl.

A Kiss for Life

I'm so in love my darling with you
My treasure trove is worth a review,
Remembering times before the "I do."
As when kissing, missing our curfew.

That kiss in shadows as first our lips met
Is one I'm sure we'll never forget –
But captured over and over, still yet,
Today's the future, I'm in your debt.

What more to life can we ask or dream
Than loving our way with eyes agleam,
To better places all faults to redeem
Retaining love as God's uppermost theme.

My love is pure untainted by fear
My heart's enflamed as I hold you Dear
My soul remains dependently near
My mesmerized spirit never will veer.

The world around us spins ever so fast
This cancer pulls our breath in a gasp,
Prevailing love remains to the last
Forever conjoined our die is cast.

This was real, the church and the kiss in Salisbury, Md. See true story at Jack's Potpourri, Note #9

Many Nuances of Sweetness

The word sweet is simply inadequate
To capture the full measure of your worth,
Intrinsically hidden as the earthquake
Erupting demonstrably from its berth.
No doubt 'sweets' inhabit your DNA –
Yet, innate assets such as these simply
Cannot account for the fragrant spray
Awash with effortless spontaneity
What attributes best convey said sweetness?
Some conjure malleable or milquetoast
Or merely kind gentle, sans weakness
Of the heart, is this one God loves the most?
Is sweetness like beauty in beholders' eyes
Is perception of either arbitrary?
While viewers seek where its richness lies
Our biases prove the true adversary.
The virtues of sweetness can't be measured
Directly: kindness, caring for others, love
Comprise one recipe that must be treasured
Endowed by our heavenly Father above.
True sweetness reaches every cell inside:
Enriching, encircling, and engaging
Each molecule of goodness we can't hide.
A simple formula that's so amazing –
But coded singularly to our heart's core
A blossoming bouquet intrinsic to You,
Exploding outward from Your bosom sore
For all to share the morning light of You.
That truth for me, as untrained observer,
Indulging tools important to me

Are traits of love that ignite my fervor.
Apportioned to bond us immortally.
Irrelevant are theories of beholders
For sweetness and beauty blend superbly.
Pure icons of positivity holders –
A hallmark You impart most ably.
Your sweetness features many layers
Complex, beguiling, flush with nuance
Washing over me and supporting players,
Evoking a rapturous renaissance.

"Beauty is not in the face; beauty is a light in the heart." Kahlil Gibran

The Smile That Waves

Amidst blue waters and foamy white caps
Obliquely crashing waves on each other,
Extending their power as each collapse
Reforming for us later to discover
A sense of ebb and flow; their rise and fall.
Incongruous with calm seas and sunny skies
A metaphor for life caught in a squall,
An exercise of power no one denies.
Your curling smile like the furl of a wave
Embraces its shore in the effort to meet
A destiny sought to cherish and save
A life immersed in diseases replete.
There's power and flow to your cherished smile
And charm enough to change reality –
Retreating briefly, thoughts to reconcile.
Expunging fear, creating fantasy
In a place scratching our names in the sand
As cascading waves uncoil tranquility,
Conspiring sweetly as triumph may demand
To capture natures best impossibility.

"We shall never know all the good that a simple smile can do." Mother Theresa

Leave Nothing in Reserve

Recall memories of Hercules
A demigod with unparalleled strength
A sense of justice and longing to please,
His human side abandoned him at length.
The lessons are told of virtues he held
Accepting punishments for sins engaged,
Unveiling mental toughness, none withheld;
Laid everything on the line, a soul uncaged.
In modern terms, he left nothing to yield.
Determined actions of value and virtue
A Metaphor: "leaving it all on the field."
Thwart paralysis: let passion burst through
Proceed into the arena of life.
Crush naysayers; defeat the moral foes
Most 'specially in raging times of strife
With a fervor only the soul bestows.
God gifted me this hue of endurance
Maturing from sports into daily life.
A sprinkle of courage and perseverance
Inspires me to spend them on my wife.
A life engraved with challenges galore
Bereft ambitions of laying it on the line,
Denies the recipe that makes love pure
My life absent that drive? I humbly decline.

IN LOVING MEMORY OF

My Mom, Dad and two Brothers, the latter of whom passed away within sixty days of each other, remain a part of me; ensconced in memories, both happy and sad. My parents both died of cancer as well as Dad's father. Two of my three brothers, unhealthy from their forties on, both passed away from complications arising from many years of chronic diabetes. In fact, brother Bob had been on the kidney transplant list for about five years and on a dialysis machine for much of that time. All four Stevenson brothers had or have diabetes believed to have been genetically passed from our paternal Grandmother, skipping a generation. It's a sobering thought to near instantaneously being "upgraded" from number three son to the family's senior Stevenson. You realize how very suddenly you change from feeling safe in life to vulnerable. So far, I've lived longer than both parents and close to exceeding the age of both brothers when they passed.

Next, you see portraits of Debbie's Dad and her maternal Grand-mother, with whom Debbie was very close, and visited everyday after elementary school days. From her school a few blocks away Debbie would walk there until picked up by her working Mom, Sweetie.

Jacqueline "Lynn" Patricia Stevenson
1925 – 2000
Chicago, Illinois
Ovarian Cancer

Joseph "Steve" Garrick Stevenson
1917 – 1987
Cape Charles, Virginia
Pancreatic Cancer

James "Jim" Casey Stevenson
1945 – 2019
Salisbury, Maryland
Diabetes (Heart)

Robert "Bob" Bratten Stevenson
1947 – 2019
Salisbury, Maryland
Diabetes

James "Jim" Albin Swaney
1916 – 2013
Norfolk, Virginia
Chronic Obstructive Pulmonary Disease (COPD)

Emma Lou Garrick (1888 – 1971)
Benjamin Bratten Stevenson (1990 – 1951)
Cape Charles, Virginia
Brain Cancer

Ursula Mary Bailey
1896-1973
Mt. Vernon, Maryland
Colon Cancer

Our Sweet Same Litter English Cocker Spaniels
Jake (left) 1986 – 2000 Brain Cancer
Ginger 1984 – 2004 Old Age

JACK'S POTPOURRI

1. The poems in Part I are not arranged in the order written and presented to Debbie daily, as my file was arranged alphabetically, not temporally. I began with my strategy of card giving sometime in May 2019 after her March diagnosis and continued that daily to the end, some 220 cards. I sprinkled a few poems in the early months until about mid-August. After Debbie's second chemo infusion, I decided to see if I had the wherewithal to "perform" daily with poems: compose, type, cut out and paste into the empty space on each card. The eighty plus poems published in Part I represent a continuous flow to the last day of her radiation protocol, an exhausting twice a day event. I chose not to include about fifteen poems due to their brevity and my decision to illustrate every poem. Illustrations for such brief verses didn't satisfy my publishing layout scheme.

2. Why illustrate? I became enamored with this feature after owning an illustrated version of Emily Dickinson's works. While my book in no way mimics the softness of the Dickinson's illustrations, different subject matter and artistry aside, the color and variety of presentation really intrigued me and captured my imagination. Of course, this book was published many years after her death, and consists, it appears, entirely of photographs, wonderfully

blended with her poems. I began not knowing how many poems I might want to illustrate, thinking much less than you have seen, one per poem; in some cases, even more than one per poem. After about 50 delivered digital paintings, working with a single illustrator, her extraordinary talent (Sheryl Chieng-Malaysia) led me to want to go all the way. It was nearly a bridge too far, as it was my responsibility to "design" each illustration that was then re-created as a digital painting in high resolution for printing.

In nearly all cases, the baseline for these paintings began with selecting a theme I wanted to emphasize. Then research began to find the best fit after scanning in some cases several hundred royalty free images I purchased from multiple internet sites. For example, Shutterstock advertises 340 million stock images. Any one search topic might have literally brought up tens of thousands of images that included photos, cartoons or vector images. Some of my search terms yielded zero, or only a handful of images. In the majority of cases, I would give my artist up to a half-dozen changes I sought, often adding other purchased images I wanted incorporated organized around the selected theme. For my first eighty-six illustrations, I provided five such concepts/images to my artist each month. Many times, she delivered the original digital watercolor painting to me before I was ready with the next five. Of course, occasionally, revisions slowed the process down. Over time I learned, especially after using other freelance sites like Fiverr. com, that artists offer scaled packages with escalating options such as size, quality, number of revision and time to complete. I have been bowled over with the talent that exist around the world and feel fortunate to have tapped into this pool of extraordinary talent.

3. My style of poetry. More than you ever wanted to know. For some reason I cannot fathom, I began writing poetry, only for Debbie, early in our marriage. Very intermittingly, spur of the moment, for special birthdays and anniversaries. While I cannot say I began writing during Debbie's illness with perfect meter (imperfect yes) in mind, I did concentrate on rhyme. Not being an experienced professional poet, together with an aggressive daily writing goal, it was impractical, no impossible, for me to have achieved even modest success on that front. I did enjoy the challenges of rhyme. As you obviously have noticed all of my poems do, in fact, rhyme using multiple schemes. Any poet (or aspiring poet) can invent their own rhyme scheme, yet there are about thirty notable most-seen schemes. ("Rhyme Scheme", n.d.) As my mechanics improved (yes indeedy) I came to immensely enjoy scribbling out a perfect (seldom) iambic pentameter verse. Of the thirty most common schemes I employed about eight including: Couplet, Tercet, Monorhyme, Quatrain, Terza Rima, Simple 4-line, Chain and Sonnet. (Ibid.)

The meter I used, at least in the beginning, could not be called consistent nor pure. Literally a work in progress, I attempted generally to follow an iambic meter of varying length. As time passed and I became more interested to improve my poetry in a more classical sense, I adopted an iambic preference, mostly of the pentameter (10 syllable) form but some shorter as well. My technique improved to a point where many of my later poems hit the mark pretty consistently. Shakespeare is well known for his use of this meter, albeit sans rhyme. Such form is called blank verse. Poetry without rhyme nor meter defines free verse. Since the early twentieth century, the majority of published lyric poetry has been written in free verse. (Poetry Foundation, n.d.) Personally, I prefer poetry of the form that contains both meter and rhyme, called formal verse, however limited my talent. I reference my earlier comment about my potential.

4. If you only looked at the "pretty pictures" then you noticed how many times a beautiful woman appears. You might not have detected that all but one (A Game You Cannot Lose) of these women are Debbie, front, back and silhouette. Of course, since I used a number of different artists and presented each with a photo of Debbie, many taken at different ages, the renditions are not all alike. That was intentional, wanting to showcase Debbie's appearance over much of her life. And of course, every boy or man is yours truly. (Exception: Share Your Burden)

5. The illustration on the front cover may raise some eyebrows. My daughter, Jaime, asked "will mom be okay with that?" My guess would be that if a woman is to have her picture on the front of a book, perhaps she'd rather it not be in a full headwrap. I frankly don't know the answer. But I'll justify my decision by saying this is the most representative photo of her throughout nine months of treatment. She's beautiful, wholesome, happy, energetic and confident. Other than hair loss, one would never know she was undergoing a heinous time. And one look at this cover tells the reader much more than words could convey. It captures cancer, beauty, resilience, poetry and that I played a loving role, one subservient to the protagonist, Debbie.

6. One of my greatest pleasures in putting this manuscript together were relationships I experienced with my artists over two years,

dialogue only of course. I partnered with some eighteen or so artists around the world, as previously mentioned. In several cases, I gently attempted to get to know them. Not their life story, just a little. For each order (146) I provided the details of my painting requirement and generally sent the corresponding poem from which the painting theme emerged. In most cases, there followed a series of communications ensuring the artist completely understood what I wanted. Of course, I always started the ball rolling after a few deliveries, by asking questions like "where did you learn to 'speak' such terrific English?" or "are you a full-time artist?" In one instance I mentioned that in America there is an expression often associated with the profession, "starving artists;" my intent to discover how hard it was for artists to thrive in their particular part of the world. For my artist in Malaysia, a resounding yes was the response. It appears a universal axiom that no matter where they live, making a living by art only is tough.

Some of the artists began opening up to me and I became very aware that as an American, I might be in a position to influence how a number of people from a dozen different countries viewed Americans through their experiences with me. None had been to American before. I could not know how many, if any, Americans they had communicated or worked with before me. Was that arrogant of me? Perhaps. Yet, I never forgot the novel *The Ugly American*, written in 1958 by William Lederer and Eugene Burdick. Living with my family in three different countries in both Asia and Europe and visiting many others, I developed a sensitivity relating to the theme of this novel. It depicted the failures of the U.S. diplomatic corps in Southeast Asia whose insensitivity to local language, culture, and customs and refusal to integrate were in marked contrast to the polished abilities of Eastern Bloc (primarily Soviet) diplomacy and led to Communist diplomatic success overseas (Meyer, 2009). John F. Kennedy was so impressed with the book that he sent a copy to each of his colleagues in the United States Senate. When he became president two years later, one of his first actions influenced by this book, was to create the Peace Corps (Ibid.)

With this in the forefront of my mind and sensing the difficulties of a career as a freelance internet artist, I wanted to be regarded as trustworthy, human and generous. After a few deliveries under my belt with the same artists after which I wrote excellent reviews and generously tipped, I could feel some loosening up on their part. I came to appreciate just how much they needed the work, relied on exceptional ratings and really desired to perform extraordinarily well in my eyes, and truly for all clients. While not sure of my expectations at the outset, I began receiving what I considered extraordinary paintings. The talent around-the-world, and I expect the reader will agree, is magnificent. I began to feel like an informal ambassador of the United States with a responsibility to project the most favorable representation of a normal average citizen. Not only did I rate the seller, but they provided comments on me, the buyer, after each purchase. I was humbled by many kind comments they posted, satisfied that my memory of *The Ugly American* and its lessons served me well.

Those from which I received five or more paintings and with whom I feel a connection, will receive a copy of this book, gratis of course. I asked for physical addresses and all provided. A few asked before I offered. It may be, and I don't know for certain, that none have been published via printed manuscripts. If not, I sincerely pray that their partnership with me by way of formal publication helps pave the way for an even greater future. I know I mentioned each by name in Acknowledgments, but I repeat my gratitude to this great dedicated group of talented artists who added a touch of class, variety and interest to my magnum opus.

7. *Merriam-Webster's Collegiate Dictionary* primary definition of a poet is "one who writes poetry." By that definition I am a poet. On a much more in-depth scale, William Wordsworth (1770-1850), considered the father of the romantic age of English literature wrote perhaps the most comprehensive commentary on the characteristics and responsibilities of both poets and poetry in his *Preface to Lyrical Ballads (1802).* He wrote:

> "What is a Poet? To whom does he address himself? And what language is to be expected from him? He is a man speaking to men: a man, it is true, endued with more lively sensibility, more enthusiasm and tenderness, who has a greater knowledge of human nature, and a more comprehensive soul, than are supposed to be common among mankind; a man pleased with his own passions and volitions, and who rejoices more than other men in the spirit of life that is in him; delighting to contemplate similar volitions and passions as manifested in the goings-on of the universe, and habitually impelled to create them where he does not find them. To these qualities he has added a disposition to be affected more than other men

by absent things as if they were present; an ability of conjuring up in himself passions, which are indeed far from being the same as those produced by real events, yet (especially in those parts of the general sympathy which are pleasing and delightful) do more nearly resemble the passions produced by real events, than anything which, from the motions of their own minds merely, other men are accustomed to feel in themselves; whence, and from practice, he has acquired a greater readiness and power in expressing what he thinks and feels, and especially those thoughts and feelings which, by his own choice, or from the structure of his own mind, arise in him without immediate external excitement." (Wordsworth, 1802)

Without reservation, within the all-encompassing description of a poet. (and despite "men" only reference, ignorant of later recognition that the first poet might have been a woman), I again reiterate "I cannot claim to be a true poet." Let's take a short walk down the annals of history to apply even more context to the representation of poets. Back to the very beginning. For the history buffs reading this no less. The framework of this art medium goes back beyond 4,000 years. Little known Enheduanna, daughter of the first to build an empire, King Sardon, was born around 2179 BC and for forty years served as princess and the high priestess of a temple in what we now call southern Iraq. Enheduanna has the distinction of being the earliest known poet whose name has been recorded. The British Archaeologist Sir Leonard discovered her by accident in the ancient Sumerian city of UR in 1927. Enheduanna's poems, and edited hymnals may have taught other women at the temple how to write. Works of hers were published in English beginning in the 1960s (Rothenberg, 2021).

Then, circa 2150 – 1400 BC, *The Epic of Gilgamesh* emerged in tablet form. It consisted of forty-two Sumerian poems by unknown authors. The originals were thought to have been passed down orally from one generation to the next until inscribed tablets were recorded some 700 years later (Mark, 2018). Advance to the father of English literature and by extension, poetry, Geoffrey Chaucer, whose *Tales of Canterbury* (c. 1380 – 1400 AD) employed ten syllable verses. It is considered the forerunner of modern iambic pentameter meter. Many of us were introduced to Chaucer as well as Homer's *Iliad* and *Odyssey* in high school literature class.

There are many lists of the most influential poets in history. Forgive me if the following don't include your choices. One of these compilations includes poets such as Shakespeare, Wordsworth, Longfellow, Tennyson, Keats, Dickinson, Whitman, Poe...the list goes on. And I haven't even mentioned more modern poets like Frost and Angelou. I daresay most of us today recognize far more names of the great poets of the past than we do of poets in say the last century or so. American's "fireside poets" including Longfellow, Bryant, Whittier, Lowell and Holmes are familiar popular names because their poetry was a source of entertainment for families gathered around the fireplace, bereft of today's barrage of media disrupters.

My priority in writing centers foremost on the message I am trying to convey; format, meter-the technical aspects etc., always secondary. Publishing a book of poetry has not changed my opinion. As a generality, at least good poets are brilliant technicians and masters of imagery. I acknowledge that with the dawn of the internet there are many websites where "poets" publish their works. For me, I will stick to my viewpoint, that there is more to poetry than hanging one's sign on the door that reads "poet." In reality, most poets today have day jobs, leaving their poetry writing to after hours and postings on special poetry-oriented websites. In no way do I mean to disparage self-named poets, poet wannabes, fledgling poets or anyone who desires to be called poet. For me, it's like installing an automated putting green strip in my living room and claim to be a golfer. Perhaps poetry is "in the eyes of the beholder." Yes?

8. Anecdote: (Poem, Fruits of Labor) We have some good friends, call them Dennis and Jane. For several years at the beginning of our friendship, I raved about Debbie's homemade strawberry rhubarb pie, our family's favorite-bar none. Finally, we had them over for dinner and dessert. Pie was served for our friends and me, and we retreated to the family room to begin eating the long-awaited favorite family treat. I couldn't wait to see the expressions on their faces savoring this slice of heavenly delight. Debbie had not joined us yet. Each of us took our first bite. I immediately recognized something was seriously amiss, then glanced over at Jane and Dennis. While bereft of odious expression, their faces were oddly neutral; I thought at first. Dennis remarked "yeah! Well, this is certainly something," obviously trying to create a positive vibe. Debbie entered with her pie in hand, all smiley faced, sat, and took a bite and followed immediately with "eww...OMG." The cook just validated my own taste buds. She fessed up immediately

"Oh no, I forgot the sugar." We all had a great laugh and were relieved to know we had good cause for owning our thoughts on the deliciousness of the effort. Would you believe what occurred next? Debbie grabbed up all pies, flew to the kitchen where she sliced off the top crust and doused each piece with a healthy dose of sugar, then gently replacing the crust. Thus, restoring the pies to vestiges of the sought-after epicurean pleasure. Too crazy not to be true!

9. Anecdote. (Poem, A Kiss for Life) While it is not, this could be an actual photo. This is the exact church in Salisbury, MD where in the fall of 1963, while attending a Friday night dance in a local church hall, Debbie and I went for a stroll on a beautiful starlit night. I happened to spot this small church alcove and thought it would be a perfect place to stop and "talk." Well mostly. It was our first kiss, captured perfectly by my wonderful artist, Sheryl. At the time, the church (1887) was called Asbury Methodist Church, later renamed Faith Community Church and remains so today. The expression "a picture is worth a thousand words," has never had more truth nor meaning. Credit my great longtime friend, Connie Fries, living in Salisbury for finding this church based on my description "couple blocks from the dance, stone with an alcove and steeple." She snapped pictures which I sent to my artist.

10. Anecdote. (Poem, Angelic Disposition) Relevance? Humor with history. I grew up with a fear of squirrels. As a young boy our home had a humongous hickory tree, home to many long-tail rodents. Dad was afraid I might attempt friendship and get bitten by a rabid squirrel. He instilled a great fear in me of a horrible death

by rabies or some other rodent disease, if bitten. I carried this fear into adulthood. While serving at Ft. Bragg, North Carolina, as commander of an Army unit with 1,100 Soldiers and their 700 hundred wives, Debbie shared my private fear with her officer wife's club ladies, who I'm sure had a hearty laugh. It became widely known and at my farewell party, to my horror, I was presented a furry toy squirrel as a gag gift. I was naturally forced to "enjoy" the laugh along with the audience. Fortunately, my career did not suffer, and I have since outgrown my fears.

11. Lastly, lest anyone believes I hope to make a buck (seriously, from two orders?) from selling this book, I don't. It was and still is the farthest thought from my mind. And that hasn't changed. Only because the publisher's package I selected included the feature of retail sales online do I mention it at all. My intent has always been to create a gift for Debbie, share with close friends and family, and in the process, hopefully, create a legacy for future family generations. The profit on any books that might sell will be donated to charity, after consultation with Debbie. It's highly doubtful the proceeds will fund a new hospital wing bearing my name. Oprah? Are you interested?

EPILOGUE

It is February 2022. Clearly, I missed my goal of presenting a finished book to Debbie on our 50th anniversary. As I approached that occasion, it was clear I would miss my target. While Debbie knew of my effort, as the PayPal bills continued, she did not know my precise intent for completion nor presentation. I won't go into the many factors that influenced the slip. Suffice to say there were many, technical and non-technical.

Twenty-Seven months have passed since Debbie's final radiation therapy, completing all the medical requirements on which her team acted. Shortly thereafter, Covid-19 crept among us, and anything normal closed down. Our hopes for erasing 2019 with trips and visits with family vanished, as with all Americans. So, we hunkered down and concentrated on getting the most out of each day. I began my march toward publication over the winter and when spring hit next, we plunged ourselves into our garden, and the soon to be 160 lovely roses bushes, amongst other horticultural delights on our property. I continue to marvel in awe as Debbie's energy levels increased along with her capacity to take care of Sweetie. Other than normal daily care and ablutions, she makes sure to spend an hour or two playing cards games (Go Fish is not one of them), and board games, which

Sweetie thrives on, winning more than fifty percent of the time. Possibly more like seventy-five percent. During Debbie's treatments I witnessed much chit-chat and so much laughter as love poured from both. I believe in my heart that Debbie's love and care of Sweetie is one of, if not the deciding factor, Sweetie is still with us. Well, that and amazingly good health. I know a number of my poems captured this relationship as it was part of our daily life. Advance two more years, and there has been no slowing down, perhaps a spec as Sweetie approaches 103. I might add that Debbie has her own impressive playbook, which in my humble opinion includes a version of *leaving it all on the field* that makes my own look like child's play; as a mother, wife, daughter and friend to all.

Two days before I penned this, Debbie got the call from her oncologist with the results of nearly a day's long testing schedule of MRIs and full body nuclear scans she undergoes every six months. Normally done yearly, as was the case after completion of treatments in 2015, without clear surgical margins achieved in round two, she qualifies for six months testing intervals. Now cleared for the fourth six-month interval, we cheered the results and thank the Lord for every day we have to enjoy the love of family, friends and this beautiful planet.

Below, I had the opportunity to add a couple of poems written well after those you've seen. The first, a sonnet, presented on our anniversary, in lieu of this book, and the second one simple question answered about our good fortune. The words need no emphasis or hopefully, clarification.

Miraculous Gift

Is it conceivable
Our souls emerged even
More undefeatable
'Cause the demon was leavin'?

One soul, one heart, one goal.
Symbiotically linked
For God's purpose of soul,
We felt and never blinked.

Our lives so long ago
Received a magic gift,
Allowed our souls to glow
With momentous life shift

That's never depleted
Increasing as we age,
As cancer is defeated
We praise the Lord on his stage.

Sonnet – Fifty Years of Bliss

When asked the secret of a long marriage
I simply gaze into my dearest friend's eyes
And see the truth they cannot disparage,
Inhaling the magic all recognize.
I hear sounds of her symphonic silence
The heartbeat of unconditional love,
Compelling echoes of deep benevolence
A spirit of friendship symbolic of –
The deepest strains of honor and respect
Presiding over feelings of mutual trust –
Our essence, our legacy to protect,
With heartfelt emotions as pure and just.
We see, we hear, we feel each other's soul
Beyond ourselves, making each other Whole.

NOTE: It seems apropos to present this poem even though written well after Debbie's cancer treatments in 2019. As previously addressed, I intended to present this book to Debbie on our 50th anniversary, June 12, 2021. I wrote and pasted this poem in the card and presented It that day. It captures the sentiments of the poems in the book, unpresented, a metaphor for our lives together. Its themes of "see," "hear" and "feel" have always been our connection points.

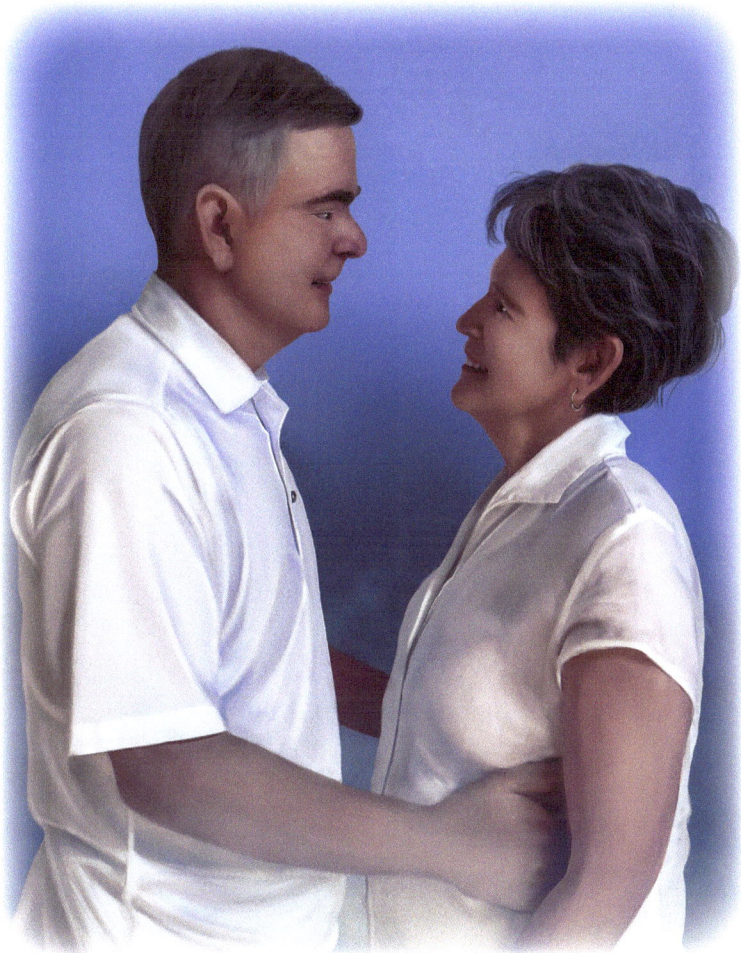

REFERENCES

Dalley, Stephanie, ed. (2000). *Myths from Mesopotamia: Creation, the Flood, Gilgamesh, and Others.* Oxford University Press. ISBN 978-0-19-953836-2.

Glossary of Poetic Terms. (2021, January 14). PoetryFoundation.Org. https://www.poetryfoundation.org/learn/glossary-terms/free-verse

Mark. Joshua. (2018). "Gilamesh." History.org. https://www.worldhistory.org/gilgamesh Meyer M. (2009). "Still Ugly After All These Years." [Review of the Book *The Ugly American,* by W. Lederer & E. Burdick]. *New York Times Book Review* https://www.nytimes.com/2009/07/12/books/review/Meyer-t.html

Poetry Foundation, Glossary of Poetic Terms: Free Verse. https://www.poetryfoundation.org/learn/glossary-terms/free-verse

Rhyme Scheme. (2021, February 22). In *Wikipedia* https://en.wikipedia.org/wiki/Rhyme_scheme#cite_note-1Rothenberg. J. (2021). "Enheduanna (2300 BCE.): Seven Sumerian Temple Hymns." Jacket2.org, https://jacket2.org/commentary/enheduanna-2300-bce-seven-sumerian-temple-hymns

Wordsworth, William, 1802. *Preface to Lyrical Ballads (1802).* University of Pennsylvania English Department. https://web.english.upenn.edu/~jenglish/Courses/Spring2001/040/preface1802.html

www.ingramcontent.com/pod-product-compliance
Lightning Source LLC
Chambersburg PA
CBHW041959090426
42811CB00030B/1952/J